MW00990944

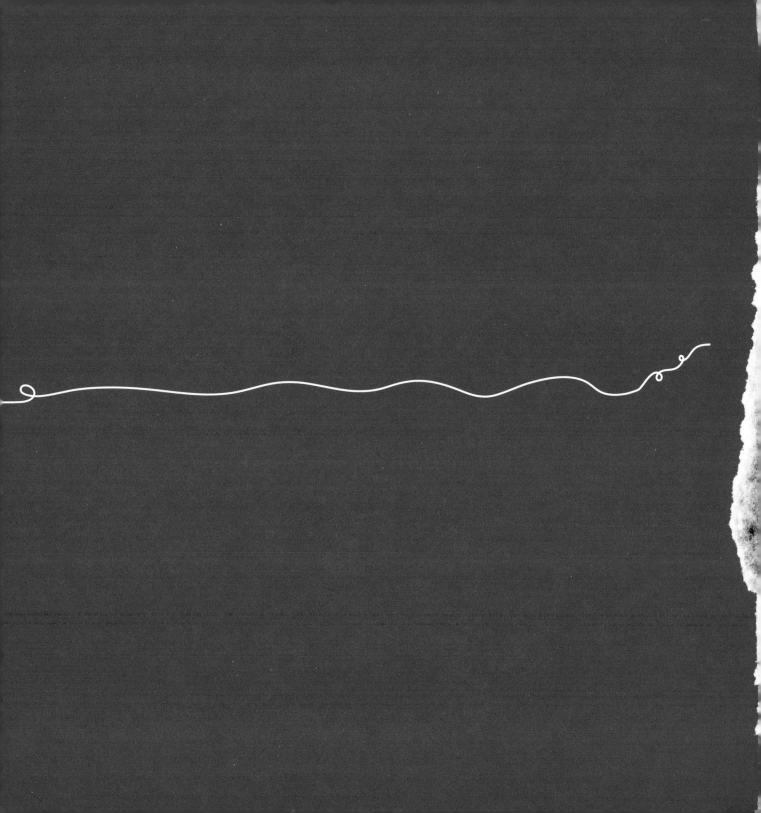

365 GREAT BIBLE STORIES

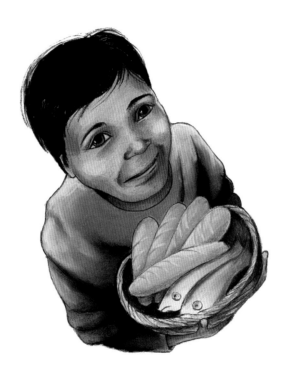

The Good News of Jesus from

Genesis to Revelation

10 9 8 7 6 5 4 3 2 1
© Copyright 2011 Carine Mackenzie

ISBN: 978-1-84550-540-0
Published by Christian Focus Publications,
Geanies House, Fearn, Tain, Ross-shire,
IV20 1TW, Scotland, U.K.
Cover design by moose77.com
Illustrations by David Lundquist
Printed in China

This book is dedicated to the Lord God who has given us the good news of
the gospel. He has given us the privilege of sharing this gospel through life,
love and literature. Our thanks are due to him and to the many children and
families who have, over the years, read these books along with us.

365 GREAT BIBLE STORIES

The Good News of Jesus from

Genesis to Revelation

Carine Mackenzie

CF4·K

How To Use This Book

In this book you will find enough stories for you to read one a day for the whole year, even if it is a leap year ... because although the book is called 365 Great Bible Stories, we've tagged on an extra story at the end.

Of course you might like to read several stories all at once and that's fine too. You might start at Genesis and go all the way through to Revelation in one sitting, or it might take you several goes.

Whatever way you want to read the truth of God's Word is fine. But it's a good thing to remember who it is you are reading about and that he has got something to say to you. The book that these stories come from, the Bible, was written by God. It has no errors in it and is absolutely truthful.

Now if you find that you want to mix things up a bit and want to read a bit differently for a change, look over at the opposite page. There you will find different themes for you to follow. Flick through the book and when you spot a lamb picture – that's a salvation story. When you spot a dove picture that's a story about the Holy Spirit. Look out for the scroll – that's going to be a story about God's Word. If you see a little road winding into the distance someone's going travelling. If you see a sword or some armour then you'll know that story has got a fight or a battle mentioned in it.

Are you ready to start? Whatever way you go – this book is about God and his ways. Follow him.

Contents

Jesus Christ and Salvation

God's Word

Wars and Battles

Themes and Topics

Travelling and Journeys

The Holy Spirit

1. Creation, the Fall, the Flood, and the Exodus

Books of the Bible:

Genesis - Exodus

What you will read about:

Creation, The Fall, Cain and Abel, Babel,
Abraham and Sarah, Hagar and Ishmael,
Isaac, Rebekah, Jacob and Esau,
Rachel and Leah, Joseph,
Moses and the Exodus.

1. God Made The World - Genesis 1

In the beginning God made the heavens and the earth. At first everything was dark and empty. God spoke, 'Let there be light.' And there was light. God called the light day and the darkness night.

On the second day God made the sky with clouds and atmosphere. God made all the water in the world.

On the third day he formed the dry land. 'Let the seas be gathered into one place and let the dry land appear,' God said. By God's powerful Word, hills and valleys were made, mountains and plains. Trees and plants, grass and flowers were made to cover the land. God saw that what he had made was good.

On the fourth day God put in place the sun, moon and stars. This gave order to the day and night. The sun gave warmth and daylight to God's world. God made all the stars in the universe. It is impossible for us to count them but God counts the stars and names each one of them. God was pleased with what he had made.

THINK: The Word of God is powerful. Jesus Christ, the Son of God, is called the Word. By him the light was produced. He is the true light, the Light of the World.

On the fifth day God made the fish and sea creatures that live in the oceans – the huge whale and the tiny shrimp – all made by God.

God also made all the birds that fly through the air – the eagle, the robin, the seagull and all the rest. God knew that what he had made was good.

On the sixth day God made all the animals. 'Let the earth bring forth living creatures,' God said and it happened by his powerful Word. God made the cattle and sheep, the lion and tiger, the mouse and snake. God saw that it was good.

THINK: When we look at all the animals, birds, insects and fish that God has made, it should help us to praise him for his wisdom and power.

The Bible tells us that there is only one God. There are three different persons in this one God, God the Father, God the Son and God the Holy Spirit. They exist together, but we must worship them as one God.

Our world was created by God. The first words of the Bible are 'In the beginning God ...' He has existed from all eternity. John speaks of the Son of God as the Word who was God and with God the Father in the beginning. The world was created by the Word that God spoke. When the world was empty and formless, God the Spirit was hovering over the waters.

So the three persons who are the one God were involved in the creation of the world and of people. 'Let us make man in our image, like ourselves,' said God, as he made the first man Adam.

This is a great mystery which should make us worship God.

PRAY: Ask God to help you to praise him. He is your Lord and God. He is so great. Ask him to help you worship him as God the Father, God the Son and God the Holy Spirit – three persons but one God.

The true God is one God but he consists of three persons – God the Father, God the Son, and God the Holy Spirit. On the sixth day God said, 'Let us make man in our image, like us.'

God made human beings to rule over the animals and to take care of the whole earth. God made Adam from the dust of the ground and he breathed life into him. God did not want Adam to be alone. He made him fall into a deep sleep and removed one of Adam's ribs. From this rib, God made a woman called Eve. She was Adam's wife and helper.

Adam and Eve were different from the animals. God gave them a living soul. God blessed them and told them to have children.

God saw everything that he had made and knew that it was very good. God rested on the seventh day. It was a day of rest for Adam and Eve too. God blessed the seventh day and made it holy.

THINK: The Lord Jesus used the Lord's Day perfectly. He wanted to please his Father. It is good for us to have one day in seven – the Lord's Day – as a special day of rest and worship.

God gave Adam and Eve a beautiful garden to live in – the Garden of Eden. In the garden were beautiful trees with tasty fruit. Adam and Eve could eat them freely. Adam worked in the garden, cultivating it and looking after it. He gave names to all the animals and birds.

Adam and Eve were perfect when they were created. They lived in perfect harmony. They were naked, but they were not ashamed. There was no sin at this time. God's whole creation was beautiful and pleasing to him.

In the middle of the garden was the tree of life and the tree of the knowledge of good and evil. 'You must not eat of the tree of the knowledge of good and evil,' God told Adam. 'If you eat the fruit from that tree, you will die.'

THINK: God loved Adam and Eve and blessed them. God is the same today. He loves his children with an everlasting love.

God had told Adam not to eat of the tree of the knowledge of good and evil.

Satan, disguised as a serpent, came to Eve in the garden.

'Did God really say you should not eat from every tree in the garden?' he asked.

'We are not to eat from the tree in the middle of the garden,' Eve replied. 'Nor touch it, or we will die.'

'You will not die,' the serpent replied. 'God knows that if you eat it you will be like him knowing good and evil.'

Eve looked at the tree and wanted to eat the fruit. It looked so good. She reached out and took some fruit and ate it. She gave some to Adam and he ate it too.

Immediately their lives changed. They realised that they were naked and sewed fig leaves together to make clothes for themselves.

THINK: Adam and Eve were taken in by the lies of Satan, God's enemy. He still tries to trick God's people but God is much stronger than him.

In the evening Adam and Eve heard God walking in the garden. They hid in the trees. God called out, 'Where are you?'

'I heard you in the garden,' Adam replied. 'I was afraid because I was naked, so I hid.'

'Who told you that you were naked?' asked God. 'Have you eaten fruit from the tree that I told you not to eat?'

Adam tried to pass on the blame. 'The woman that you gave me, she gave me the fruit and I ate.'

Eve then said, 'The serpent deceived me and I ate.'

Sin had entered the world and spoiled it.

THINK: Adam and Eve sinned by eating the fruit. Then they sinned again by trying to pass the blame. One sin always leads to another.

God first spoke to the serpent. 'Because of what you have done, you will be cursed among animals. There will be enmity between you and the woman.'

God told Eve that pain would come into the world. When children were born, she would have pain.

Adam was told that the ground would be difficult to look after now. Thorns, thistles and weeds would grow. Adam would have to work very hard to grow his food.

God made clothes of animal skins for Adam and Eve. God sent Adam and Eve out of the garden. He sent cherubim with flaming swords to guard the way to the tree of life.

THINK: God has to punish sin. But he made a way of escape. When God punished the serpent – the devil – he spoke of him being defeated by the seed of the woman, Eve. This points us to Jesus who defeated the devil when he died on the cross.

Adam and Eve made their home outside the Garden of Eden. They had to work hard. Adam and Eve had two baby boys – Cain and Abel. When they grew up Abel was a shepherd and Cain grew crops.

One day they decided to give an offering to the LORD God. Cain offered some fruit and vegetables. Abel brought the very best of his sheep. God was pleased with Abel's offering but not with Cain's. Cain became very angry and jealous.

'Why are you angry?' God asked him. He knew what was in Cain's heart. 'Sin is crouching at the door like a wild animal ready to attack you. You must control it.'

Cain did not listen. When Cain and Abel were out in the field together, Cain turned on his brother and killed him. He buried his body in the ground.

'Where is your brother?' God asked.

'How should I know? Am I my brother's keeper?' snapped Cain.

God knew what Cain had done. 'You are now under a curse. You must leave the land and have no fixed home.' However, even though Cain was banished from his home God protected him.

Sin always has consequences. It causes problems and grief. Cain murdering his brother must have caused great grief to Adam and Eve too.

THINK: Abel's offering of a sheep points us to the much better sacrifice for sin – the Lord Jesus who is the Lamb of God and the perfect sacrifice for sin.

Years passed and more and more people were born. God was grieved with their behaviour. He decided to destroy all the wicked people from the world. Only Noah pleased God.

'Make an ark of gopher wood,' God told Noah. 'Make rooms in the ark and cover it in and out with tar.' God told Noah what size to make the ark – with a door, window and three decks. Noah obeyed God in every detail.

'Take two of every kind of animal,' God told him, 'and take seven of those used for food and sacrifices.'

Noah and his wife and his sons, Shem, Ham and Japheth, and their wives went into the ark – a boat in the middle of dry land. The animals went in too. God closed the door.

The rain began to fall. It rained and rained for forty days and forty nights. Floods covered the earth. The ark floated along with Noah and his family safe inside.

Just as God had warned, every living thing died – people, animals, birds, reptiles. Only those in the ark were safe. For 150 days water completely flooded the earth.

THINK: Only eight people were saved from the flood. Only those who are trusting in the Lord Jesus are safe from the destruction which our sin deserves.

God did not forget about Noah, his family and the animals in the ark.

The floodwaters gradually subsided. The ark came to a standstill on the top of Mount Ararat.

Noah's faith in God and his obedience to his Word, saved himself and his family from disaster.

Forty days later, Noah opened the window of the ark and released a raven which flew back and fore over the water.

He sent out a dove, which looked for dry land to rest on. There was still none visible so the dove came back to the ark.

Seven days later Noah sent out the dove again. This time it came back with an olive leaf in its beak. Noah knew the waters were going down.

A week later the dove left the ark and did not return. She could now live on dry land. Some weeks later when the earth had dried up, God told Noah to leave the ark, with his family. 'Let all the birds, animals and reptiles go.'

THINK: We can have faith in God when we trust him completely and believe what he tells us in his Word.

Noah worshipped God. He built an altar and sacrificed the suitable animals and birds. God was pleased with Noah. God promised, 'As long as the world exists, there will always be a planting time, and a harvest time, cold and heat, summer and winter, day and night.'

God made a special promise called a covenant with Noah and his sons. 'Never again will I destroy the whole earth with a flood, even when people do evil,' God promised.

As a sign of the promise, God showed Noah a rainbow in the sky. This reminds us too of God's promise.

God's promises are always kept. He never forgets. Many of his promises bring comfort. 'Come to me and I will give you rest. I will hear you when you pray to me. I will never leave you or forsake you.'

THINK: Some promises are warnings. The wicked will be punished. But just as Noah found safety in the ark, we can find safety in Christ Jesus.

After the great flood there was a time when everyone in the world spoke the same language.

When some people travelled east, they found a broad plain called Shinar. They decided to settle there. 'Let's build a great city here,' they said 'and make a name for ourselves. We can build a great tower that will reach right to heaven.' So they gathered together and started to build a tower with bricks and tar.

God was watching them. He knew the pride of their hearts. He knew their intentions. God decided to confuse their language. Instead of speaking the same language, the people spoke many different languages.

Chaos resulted. No one understood each other. They were completely confused. They were forced to stop building the city. The place was called the Tower of Babel because it was there that God confused the languages.

THINK: These people could never have reached heaven. God, however, reached down to earth to save sinners when his Son, Jesus, came as the Saviour.

Abraham was a wealthy man who owned many sheep, cattle, donkeys and camels. His wife, Sarah, was a beautiful woman, but she had no children.

Abraham and Sarah lived in the city called Ur in the land of Mesopotamia (now Iraq).

One day God spoke to Abraham, 'Leave your home country. Go to another land. I will show you where to go.'

God made a special promise or covenant to Abraham. 'I will make your family a great nation. I will bless you. All the peoples in the world will be blessed through you.'

Sarah and Abraham and other members of their family set off on their long journey. They travelled north for over 500 miles to Haran. They settled there for a while but God told Abraham to move on to the land of Canaan. 'I will give this land to your children,' God promised.

Abraham built an altar and worshipped God. They travelled on with Lot, their nephew. Abraham and Sarah had faith in God. They obeyed him even when it meant travelling to an unknown land.

THINK: God is faithful to his promises. The great blessing is the Lord Jesus Christ who died so that his people would have life.

Abraham was very rich with lots of animals, gold and silver. His nephew, Lot, also had many flocks of sheep, herds of cattle and servants. In fact there were so many animals belonging to Abraham and Lot that they could not find enough grass to feed them all. The herdsmen began to quarrel.

'Please do not let there be strife between your herdsmen and mine,' Abraham said to Lot. 'We are family.'

Abraham solved the problem. 'Let's part company,' he said to Lot. 'You choose where you want to go. I will go the other way.'

Lot chose the fruitful plains of Jordan to the east near the wicked city of Sodom. Abraham and Sarah went in the other direction.

God spoke to Abraham. 'Look all around the land. Your children will possess it. They will be so numerous, it will be as hard to count them as it is to count the grains of dust on the ground.'

Abraham worshipped God. When God told Abraham how great his family would be, it did not make him proud, it made him worship the LORD.

PRAY: Thank God for your family. Thank him also for the family of God – those who trust Jesus Christ. They have been adopted into God's family and are his children. How wonderful!

Abraham and Sarah were very old – eighty-five years and seventy-five years – and still they had no son. But Abraham believed God's promise.

Sarah became impatient. She decided that her maidservant would have a child for her. She told Abraham to take Hagar to be his wife. However, Sarah became so jealous of Hagar that the servant had to run away. God spoke words of comfort and promise to Hagar, 'Your son will be a great nation too.'

Hagar returned to Sarah and gave birth to a son called Ishmael. He was not the son that God had promised Abraham. God spoke again to Abraham and told him plainly that Sarah would have a son. Abraham had to laugh. He could hardly believe it.

Abraham and Sarah should not have tried to work out the situation by themselves. This caused problems in the family and in the nations later on.

THINK: God's words of comfort are so helpful when we are in trouble. He is the God of all comfort. When you are anxious, go to God's Word to help in every time of need.

One day Abraham was sitting at the door of his tent during the hottest part of the day. He looked up and saw three men close by. Abraham hurried over to welcome them.

'Come and rest. Let me wash the dust from your feet and get you something to eat.'

These were no ordinary visitors. The LORD had come with a message. Abraham rushed to the tent. 'Quick Sarah,' he said. 'Get some flour and bake some bread for our visitors.'

Some meat was cooked too and a fine meal prepared for the visitors.

'Where is your wife, Sarah?' they asked.

'Over there in the tent,' he replied.

'About this time next year Sarah will have a son.'

Sarah was listening out of sight. Sarah laughed to herself when she heard these words. She and Abraham were both so old.

'Why did Sarah laugh and doubt my words?' the LORD said to Abraham.

'I did not laugh,' Sarah lied. But the LORD cannot be deceived. 'You did laugh,' he said.

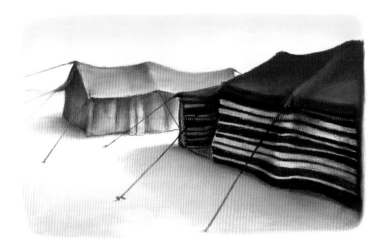

THINK: Nothing is impossible for God. We should not doubt the power of God. He is in charge of every situation.

God's promise to Abraham and Sarah was fulfilled. Sarah had a little son at the very time the LORD had said. This was a miracle. Abraham was 100 years old and Sarah was ninety. They had waited so long for a child – for the son that God had promised.

In their impatience Sarah and Abraham had tried to sort out the problem themselves. Sarah had even laughed when the LORD told her that she would have a son in a year's time – but Sarah should have realised that this wasn't a joke. There is nothing too hard for the LORD. When she held her baby son in her arms Sarah saw how true this was. She must have felt overjoyed!

Abraham called the boy 'Isaac' which means 'he laughs'.

Abraham's faith was rewarded.

THINK: Isaac's birth was a miracle. Jesus' birth was even more miraculous. He was born to a girl called Mary who did not have a husband. Angels announced his birth!

Isaac grew up strong and healthy. When he became big enough, Abraham made a big feast for Isaac. Sarah's enjoyment of the party was spoiled, however. Ishmael who was fourteen years older than Isaac, made fun of Isaac. Sarah was jealous.

'Get rid of that slave woman and her son,' she said to Abraham. 'That boy will never be an heir with my son, Isaac.'

Abraham was upset by this quarrel in his family. God told him to listen to Sarah.

So Abraham got up early in the morning and sent Hagar and Ishmael away with some bread and a skin bottle of water. They wandered about in the desert of Beersheba.

Soon the water was all used up. Hagar and Ishmael became very thirsty. Hagar thought they would die. They both started to cry.

The angel of the LORD came to Hagar. 'Do not be afraid,' the angel said. 'God has heard your boy's cries.'

God opened her eyes and she saw a well of water. They filled their bottles and drank as much as they needed.

God was with Ishmael as he grew up in the desert lands. He had promised to make him into a great nation too.

God sees every one of us. He cares and provides for our every need.

THINK: Jesus is the water of life. He is the only one who can really satisfy our deepest needs.

Isaac was Abraham and Sarah's only son. God had promised to bless their family. God tested Abraham's faith in a remarkable way.

God said to Abraham, 'Take your son, your only son, Isaac, whom you love, and go to Mount Moriah. There you will sacrifice him as an offering.'

Abraham believed in God. All things were possible with him. Early next morning, Abraham saddled a donkey and cut a large bundle of wood. He travelled for three days to Mount Moriah with Isaac and two servants. Leaving the servants at the foot of the hill, Abraham and Isaac went on together. Isaac carried the wood and Abraham took a knife and the fire.

Isaac was puzzled. 'Where will we get a lamb for the offering?' he asked.

'God will provide the lamb,' Abraham replied.

Abraham built an altar and arranged the wood on it. He tied Isaac's hands and feet and laid him on top of the wood.

THINK: Isaac carried the wood to the top of Mount Moriah. His life was spared. Jesus carried the wooden cross to Calvary, where he died for our sins.

21. Isaac is Spared - Genesis 22

Abraham believed that God was in charge. He raised up the knife ready to kill Isaac. The angel of the LORD called out, 'Abraham, Abraham!'

'Here I am,' he replied.

'Do not harm the boy,' the angel said. 'I know that you fear God because you were willing to sacrifice your only son, Isaac.'

Abraham looked up and saw a ram caught by its horns in a bush. This animal was used as the sacrifice for a burnt offering.

Abraham called the name of this place Jehovah Jireh – 'The LORD will Provide'.

The angel spoke to Abraham again, telling him that God would bless him and his family.

THINK: God provided a ram for the sacrifice. But later he provided a lamb for another sacrifice. He provided Jesus Christ, the Lamb of God to be the perfect sacrifice for sin on the cross at Calvary.

Abraham called the place where the ram was sacrificed 'Jehovah Jireh'. This means 'The LORD will provide'. God had provided the ram for the sacrifice.

The LORD God is Jehovah Jireh for us too. He provides for all our needs: food, shelter, family, friends. All we have is from the LORD. The greatest thing he has provided is the Lord Jesus Christ as the sacrifice for our sins.

Many, many years later John the Baptist met Jesus and called him the Lamb of God who takes away the sin of the world (John 1:29).

Isaac was spared from giving up his life, but Jesus was not. He died on the cross as a sacrifice for sinners. Those who repent and are sorry for their sins and who trust fully in Jesus belong to him and are saved.

PRAY: Thank the LORD for every gift that he has given you. Thank him most of all for the gift of his Son, the Lord Jesus Christ, the Saviour of sinners.

Isaac needed to find a good wife. So Abraham sent his chief servant back to his homeland to find a wife for Isaac from his own people.

The servant set off with ten camels and many gifts to the city of Nahor in Mesopotamia where he stopped at a well during the evening.

'Please give me success,' he prayed to God. 'If I ask a girl for a drink of water, may the right girl offer to draw water for my camels.'

Before he had finished praying, Rebekah, the daughter of Abraham's nephew, came to the well with a jar on her shoulder. She was very beautiful. She filled her jar at the well. The servant ran up to her.

'Please let me have a drink from your jar.' She readily gave him a drink. 'I will also draw water for your camels,' she said.

When the camels finished drinking, the servant took out a gold ring and two bracelets and asked Rebekah whose daughter she was. Rebekah told him.

God had guided the servant to Abraham's relations. He bowed down and worshipped God.

THINK: God guides his people by his Word the Bible and situations and incidents he puts into our lives. Another word for this is providence.

Rebekah ran to tell her family of the visitor. Her brother, Laban, welcomed the servant into the home. Before he would eat any food, he had to explain the purpose of his visit. He told them how Abraham wanted to find a wife for his son, Isaac, from his own people and how God had guided him to Rebekah.

Laban and his father, Bethuel, realised that God himself had arranged the meeting. 'Take Rebekah to your master's son,' they said.

Abraham's servant bowed low before the LORD. He brought out more gifts for Rebekah – gold and silver jewellery and clothes and gifts for her mother and brother.

The next morning the servant wanted to set off straight away with Rebekah.

'Let her stay with us a while longer,' said her family.

'Don't make me delay,' replied the servant.

'Let's ask Rebekah what she wishes to do. Will you go with this man?' they asked.

'I will go,' replied Rebekah.

So they let her go with their blessing. Rebekah willingly left her family to follow God's purpose for her life.

PRAY: Ask the Lord to make you willing to follow the Lord Jesus. It is an important choice to follow him. Ask God to help you trust in him and obey his Word.

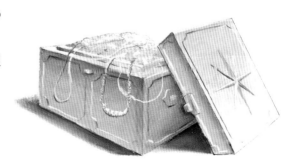

Isaac was living in the Negev desert. One evening as he was out walking and thinking, he noticed a train of camels in the distance. It was Rebekah on her way to marry him.

Rebekah noticed him and climbed down from her camel. 'Who is that man walking towards us?' she asked.

'That is Isaac, my master's son,' the servant replied.

Isaac took Rebekah as his wife. He loved her. Isaac was forty years old when he got married. Nearly twenty years passed and still no child was born. Isaac prayed about this. God answered his prayer and Rebekah became pregnant with twins. The two children struggled so much inside her that she cried out to God. 'Why am I like this?'

God explained to her, 'Two nations are in your womb. The older shall serve the younger.'

Rebekah gave birth to twins – Esau who was red and hairy and Jacob who was smooth-skinned. As they grew up they were quite different. Esau was his father's favourite, keen on hunting and an outdoor life, but Jacob preferred staying at home. His mother loved him best. This led to much heartache.

THINK: God still hears and answers prayer. The lives of Abraham, Isaac and Jacob teach us that.

One day Jacob cooked a lovely stew. Esau came in from the field, exhausted. 'Please give me some of that red stew,' he asked Jacob.

Jacob saw an opportunity for himself. 'Sell me your birthright,' he replied.

The birthright referred to the rights of the firstborn son in a Hebrew family. The oldest son would inherit a double portion of his father's property and he had special privileges and responsibilities.

'I am about to die of hunger,' replied Esau. 'Of what use will a birthright be to me?'

So he solemnly promised and sold his birthright to Jacob for some bread and lentil stew.

Esau showed no respect for his birthright. He sold it, without a thought, to satisfy his hunger.

THINK: Esau was Isaac's heir. This meant he was to inherit the family possessions after his father's death. God's people are heirs of God with Christ. We should value this great inheritance.

One day when Isaac was old and blind, he called his son, Esau. 'Take your bow and arrow and hunt for some venison. Make me a savoury stew. After I eat it, I will give you my blessing before I die.'

As Esau set off to hunt, Rebekah had overheard Isaac speaking to Esau. She wanted Jacob to receive the blessing instead. She quickly gave him some orders.

'Go and fetch two young goats from the flock. I will make some tasty stew that your father loves. Take it to him and he will bless you.'

'But Esau is a hairy man and I am smooth,' he protested. 'If my father realises I am deceiving him, he may curse me instead.'

His mother persuaded him. She put Esau's clothes on Jacob and the skins from the young goats on his hands and the smooth part of his neck. Jacob took the savoury stew to his father.

THINK: It was wrong of Rebekah to encourage Jacob to lie. God has told us not to say false things to or about other people.

Isaac thought that Esau had come back very quickly. He felt Jacob's hands – they were hairy like Esau. The voice did not seem quite right, but Jacob lied to his father, 'I am Esau,' he said.

Isaac ate the food. When Jacob came up to kiss his father, Isaac smelled Esau's clothes. So he gave his blessing to Jacob, the deceiver.

Esau came home from hunting. He brought the venison to Isaac and asked for his blessing. Isaac trembled when he realised what had happened. Esau was distraught. He hated Jacob and planned to kill him as soon as his father had died.

It is very sad how sin destroys families and friendships.

We should ask God to give us a love for each other and a love for God and his Word. God's guidance and his wisdom will help families to be truly loving to each other.

THINK: One sin leads to another. Here we have seen how lying and deception led to hatred. Every sin deserves God's anger and punishment. Only the sacrifice of the Lord Jesus can cleanse us from sin.

35

When Rebekah heard that Esau planned to kill Jacob she urged him to escape to his uncle Laban's place.

'Stay with him,' she advised, 'until your brother's anger dies down. I will send for you.'

On the journey Jacob lay down in the open air with a big stone for a pillow. As he slept, he dreamed. He saw a ladder going from earth to heaven. Angels were going up and down the ladder.

God spoke to him in the dream as he had spoken to Abraham.

'I am the God of Abraham and Isaac: I will give you this land. You and your children will be blessed. I will keep you wherever you go.'

Jacob woke up afraid and full of awe. 'This is surely the house of God and the gate of heaven.' He called the place Bethel which means 'House of God.'

Early next morning Jacob took the stone that had been his pillow, set it up as a pillar and poured oil on it. He made a vow to follow the LORD and to give him one tenth of all his income.

THINK: Even though Jacob was a cheat and a liar, God did not abandon him. He had promised to be his God. Jesus Christ has promised never to abandon his people. When you trust Jesus he will always be with you.

When Jacob drew near his uncle Laban's home, he stopped at a well where he met Rachel, Laban's daughter. Jacob helped her to draw water for her sheep. He introduced himself as Rebekah's son.

Rachel ran to tell her father who was delighted to meet his nephew. He welcomed him to his home. Jacob agreed to work for Laban for seven years, as long as he could marry Rachel. Jacob loved Rachel so much, that seven years seemed a very short time.

But Jacob the trickster, was tricked himself. On the wedding day, the bride arrived covered by a veil. When the veil was removed Jacob discovered that he had married Leah, Rachel's older sister.

'Why did you deceive me?' he demanded.

'The younger sister cannot get married before the older,' Laban insisted. 'You can marry Rachel if you work for another seven years.'

Jacob gladly did this.

THINK: God had a plan for Jacob's life – even where he would work and who he would marry. It was all under God's control. Your loving heavenly Father has a plan for your life too. Trust him to help you and guide you.

Jacob loved Rachel more than Leah. But God blessed Leah with children. Her first baby was called Reuben. Then Simeon was born. Next came Levi, and then Judah.

Rachel was envious of her sister. She complained to Jacob. Jacob answered her angrily, 'Am I God? He is the one who gives children.'

Rachel was so desperate to have a child, she asked her maid Bilhah to have a baby for her. A little boy called Dan was born to Bilhah and then another called Naphtali.

Leah gave Jacob her servant, Zilpah, as a wife. She also had two sons – Gad and Asher.

Leah had two more sons Issachar and Zebulun, and a daughter, Dinah. Then at last God remembered Rachel and answered her prayers by giving her a son. She called his name Joseph.

Jacob wanted to take his family back to his own country. Laban was not keen on the idea. He liked having Jacob working for him. God told Jacob to return to Canaan. 'I will be with you,' he promised.

THINK: Leah envied her sister because Jacob loved Rachel more. Rachel envied her sister because Leah had many babies. Contentment with our situation is a blessing from God. We should not be envious of what other people have.

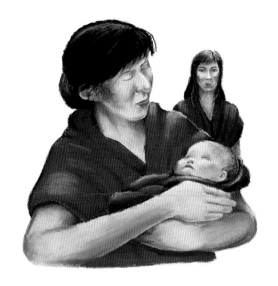

Jacob, his family, servants and animals journeyed towards Canaan. Jacob was anxious about meeting Esau again. He had treated him badly, tricking him out of his father's blessing.

One night on the journey, Jacob camped alone at the brook Jabbok. A man came to him and wrestled with him until dawn. As they wrestled, Jacob's hip was put out of joint.

'Let me go,' the man said.

'I will not let you go unless you bless me,' Jacob replied.

'Your name will no longer be Jacob (deceiver) but Israel (prince),' said the man. 'You have struggled with God and man and won.'

Jacob realised that the stranger was God. He called the place Peniel because he had seen God face to face.

After Jacob's meeting with God at Peniel, he was left with a limp. This would always remind him of his meeting with God.

PRAY: Thank the Lord that we can meet with him when we pray to him in faith. Thank him for his gift of his Son, our Saviour. Ask him to help you trust in him so that you too can have your sins forgiven.

Jacob sent servants ahead of the family with presents for Esau – goats, sheep, camels, cows, bulls, donkeys and foals – a wonderful gift.

'Tell Esau that his servant Jacob is coming behind,' he said. He prayed for the safety of himself and his family.

Jacob divided his family into groups – Bilhah and Zilpah with their children in the front, then Leah and her children, then Rachel and her son Joseph.

Jacob bowed down before Esau but Esau welcomed him with open arms. All was forgiven. The brothers were reconciled. Jacob introduced his family.

Esau did not want to take Jacob's gifts. 'I have plenty. Keep what you have.' But Jacob insisted that he accept.

They made their way safely to the land of Canaan. Jacob's prayer was answered.

THINK: God is the answerer of prayer. His answer is not always 'yes'. Sometimes he says 'no', as he is much wiser than we are. Sometimes he says, 'Wait a while,' because he knows what is good for us.

Joseph was the favourite son of his father, Jacob. He had ten older brothers, one sister and one younger brother, Benjamin. Jacob gave Joseph a beautiful multi-coloured coat to show how much he loved him. This made the older brothers jealous. They hated Joseph.

One day Joseph told his brothers about his dream. 'We were all tying up the corn into bundles in the field,' he said. 'My bundle stood up straight but yours all bowed down in front of mine.'

His brothers became even angrier. 'Do you think that we will bow down to you one day?'

Joseph had another dream. 'In my dream the sun, the moon and eleven stars all bowed down to me,' he told them.

Did this mean he would be more important than all his family? His brothers hated him even more.

THINK: Favouritism caused problems in Jacob's family. It led to jealousy and other sins. When you feel jealous, ask God to help you to be loving and forgiving.

While Joseph's brothers were looking after the sheep far away from home, Jacob decided to send Joseph to see how they were getting on.

The brothers noticed Joseph in the distance. Together they plotted to kill him. 'What will his dreams mean then?' they gloated.

One brother, Reuben, said, 'Don't kill him. Just throw him into the pit.'

So Joseph's beautiful coat was torn from him and he was flung into a horrible dark pit. Reuben planned to rescue Joseph later but while he was elsewhere some merchants came along on their way to Egypt. Brother Judah had an idea. 'Let's sell Joseph as a slave to these merchants. We will make some money. It would not be good to kill our own brother.'

Joseph was pulled out of the pit and sold for twenty pieces of silver to the merchants. Soon he arrived in Egypt as a slave.

THINK: Joseph was betrayed by his brothers, but it was all part of God's plan. The Lord Jesus was betrayed by Judas, one of his disciples. But God's plan for salvation was still in place.

The brothers told lies to Jacob so that he believed a wild animal had eaten Joseph. He was heartbroken. But Joseph was alive and working for Potiphar, an important captain in Pharaoh's army.

God was with Joseph all the time. He worked well and Potiphar rewarded him for his good work and trusted him. Potiphar's wife told lies about Joseph, accusing him of a wicked deed which he had not done at all. Potiphar believed his wife and had Joseph thrown into prison. God was with Joseph in prison too.

THINK: Nothing can separate us from the love of God. Even when life is tough, God is still with us.

Joseph was in prison with a butler and a baker who used to work for Pharaoh. One night they both had a dream which troubled them.

'God will help me to give you the meaning of these dreams,' said Joseph.

Joseph told the butler that in three days he would have his old job back. The baker, however, would die. Both dreams came true.

'Please tell Pharaoh about me,' said Joseph to the butler, as he left to go back to the palace. 'He might get me out of prison.' But the butler forgot all about Joseph.

Two years passed and still Joseph was in prison. But God was still with Joseph. Then Pharaoh himself had two dreams. Who would tell Pharaoh the meaning of them?

THINK: The butler forgot about Joseph, but God did not forget about him. God never forgets us at any time.

Pharaoh's dreams were about cattle and about ears of corn. He did not know what they meant. His wise men could not tell him either. Pharaoh was troubled.

Suddenly the butler remembered Joseph. 'I know a man in prison,' he told Pharaoh, 'who was able to tell me the meaning of my dream and the baker's dream too.'

Pharaoh sent immediately for Joseph. Joseph shaved and dressed and went to see Pharaoh.

'God will give you an answer,' he said.

Joseph explained the dreams. 'God is telling you that there will be seven years of plenty in the land, followed by seven years of famine.'

Joseph gave Pharaoh good advice. 'Find a wise man to organise the crops that are grown during the seven years of plenty. He should store part of the crop to use later when food is scarce.'

THINK: God gave Joseph the wisdom he needed to advise Pharaoh. God tells us to ask him for wisdom when we need it (James 1:5).

Pharaoh needed to find a wise man who could organise and plan.

'Since God has made my dreams known to you, Joseph,' said Pharaoh, 'I can think of no one more suitable for this task. You will be in charge of my palace. Only I will be above you in rank.'

Pharaoh gave Joseph this important job – Prime Minister. He gave him a ring for his finger, beautiful clothes and a gold chain round his neck.

Joseph had a chariot to ride in. He was a very important man.

Joseph got married and had two little boys.

When the famine came, the people were told to go to Joseph for help. People came from all over to get bread.

THINK: Joseph can often remind us of Jesus. The people came to Joseph to get bread. We should come to Jesus for the bread of life – himself.

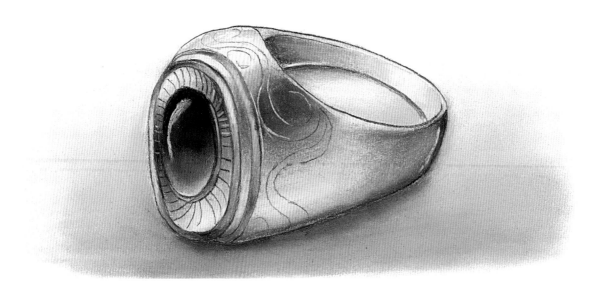

One day ten of Joseph's brothers arrived to buy bread. They fell down before the important ruler of Egypt to ask for food, not realising that he was their brother Joseph. Joseph's dreams had come true.

Joseph recognised his brothers but he did not tell them who he was. He spoke roughly to them, 'You are spies.'

'Oh, no,' they replied. 'We have come to buy food. We are brothers. Our youngest brother is at home with our father.'

'One of you go and fetch him then,' said Joseph. 'I'll keep the rest of you in prison.'

So he put them in prison for three days. Then he let them out to go back home to fetch Benjamin, on condition that one brother stayed behind in prison.

Joseph overheard his brothers speaking among themselves.

'We are being punished for our treatment of our brother, Joseph.'

They did not realise that Joseph understood their language perfectly.

THINK: Joseph's brothers remembered that they had done wrong. We all have a conscience which gives us troubled feelings when we do wrong. The only remedy is to ask God for forgiveness through the Lord Jesus Christ.

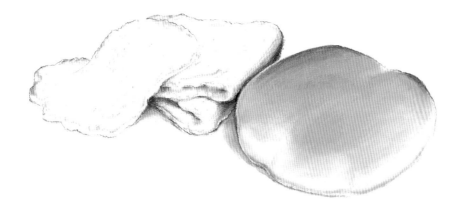

Simeon remained in Egypt while the rest returned home with the grain. To their surprise their money was found in the sacks too.

At home their father was amazed at their story. He did not want to part with Benjamin. But eventually food ran short again. They would have to go back to Egypt for more supplies.

'Benjamin will have to come too. We will look after him,' they promised.

Reluctantly Jacob agreed. 'Take the man some presents. Make sure you have double money to make up for last time,' was their father's advice.

The brothers returned to Egypt and this time Benjamin was with them. Joseph was delighted to see his young brother. He invited them all to his home for a feast. Simeon was brought out of prison. All the brothers again bowed down to Joseph.

THINK: Do you remember the dreams that Joseph had? God had fulfilled these dreams and given honour to Joseph. This is another sign that God always keeps his promises. We can rely on him.

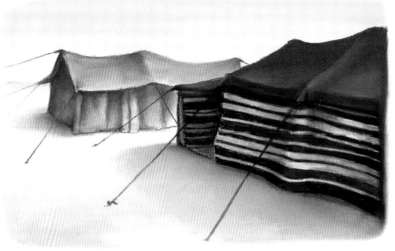

Joseph gave the order to his servant. 'Fill the men's sacks with corn, put this money back in the sacks again and put my silver cup in the sack belonging to the youngest man.'

So the brothers set off for home. Soon some of Joseph's men came chasing after them, accusing them of stealing Joseph's silver cup.

'We would never do that. You can kill whoever has a silver cup in his sack. Search us all!' they boldly exclaimed.

What a shock when the cup was found in Benjamin's sack. They returned to Joseph in a terrible state. What would happen now?

Judah said to Joseph. 'Punish me instead. Please let him go back to his father. It would kill him if anything happened to Benjamin.'

The brothers had passed Joseph's test.

PRAY: Ask the Lord to help you to be honest and truthful every day and to remember that he sees you all the time. God knows what you are doing and thinking all the time.

Joseph could not hide it any longer. He had to tell them who he was. He sent all the servants out of the room. 'I am Joseph,' he said. 'Is my father still alive?'

The brothers could not answer. They were so surprised and troubled.

'Come near,' Joseph said. 'I am your brother whom you sold to Egypt. Do not be unhappy or angry with yourselves. God sent me here to save many lives and to save your lives.

'Go back and fetch our father. You can all live here in this country.'

He kissed them and wept. His brothers then were able to talk to him.

THINK: God sent Joseph to Egypt to save his brothers from death by starvation. God sent his Son, the Lord Jesus, to save his people from eternal punishment due for their sins.

Joseph sent his brothers back to fetch his father and all the family. Big carts carried everyone and lots of food and gifts.

'Do not quarrel on the way home,' he warned them.

When they told their father, Jacob, the good news he could not believe it. They told him all that Joseph had said. When he saw the big carts sent to fetch him, he finally believed them.

'I will go and see my son, Joseph, again before I die,' he said.

After the long journey to Egypt, Jacob again met Joseph. They hugged each other and wept for a long time. Joseph's family was given the best land to settle in and they prospered there.

After their father died, Joseph's brothers were afraid that he would turn against them. But he showed kindness to them.

'Do not be afraid,' he said. 'You intended to harm me, but God intended it for good – to save many lives.'

THINK: The Good News for us is that Jesus is alive, his death on the cross defeated sin and because of this we can have eternal life through him.

During Joseph's life many difficult things happened – he was thrown in a pit, sold as a slave, falsely accused and sent to prison.

Yet all through these hard times God was at work in Joseph's life, guiding and protecting and using these events to ensure that at some point in the future Joseph would be in the right place at the right time. Joseph the slave became Joseph the Prime Minister and the one man in Egypt in charge of food supplies. God's planning, as always, was perfect as Joseph came to power before the famine and was able to stockpile food for the future. If it hadn't been for God's perfect plan in the life of Joseph, the country of Egypt, and Joseph's family, would have faced a bleak future without any food.

THINK: At first Joseph's life looked like a disaster but God meant it all for good. If we think about Jesus on the cross, we see sadness, pain and loneliness. But God used these events to provide salvation and eternal life for all who trust in him.

The Israelite people had become slaves in Egypt. The new Pharaoh was very cruel. He was afraid that the Israelites would become more powerful than him. He forced them to make bricks with water and earth mixed with chopped straw. This was then pressed into moulds. It was backbreaking work. Working in the fields was hard too. Cruel slave-masters made their work so unpleasant.

Still the Israelites multiplied and spread and Pharaoh became more anxious. Then he gave a very cruel order indeed. All the baby boys must be killed at birth. But the nurses who helped the mothers feared God and did not obey Pharaoh.

He gave the order to all the people. 'Every boy that is born must be thrown into the River Nile.'

THINK: Even in times of great hardship, God is always with his people. Persecution and trouble will never separate us from the love of Christ Jesus.

Amram and Jochebed lived in Egypt with their daughter Miriam, and son, Aaron. When another little boy was born they had to keep the baby hidden. After three months it became difficult to keep him quiet.

Jochebed thought of a plan. She made a basket of bulrushes and covered it with tar to keep it watertight. She put the baby in the basket and floated it at the edge of the River Nile. Miriam kept watch to see what would happen.

Pharaoh's daughter, the princess, came to bathe in the river. She noticed the basket in the reeds. When she saw the baby crying, she took pity on him. Miriam came out of hiding. 'Shall I fetch a nurse for you?' The princess agreed. So Miriam ran for her mother. Now Jochebed could look after her baby without fear.

The princess adopted the baby, giving him the name 'Moses', which means 'drawn out of the water'.

THINK: Jochebed's clever plan, Miriam's watchful eye and the princess's compassion were all used by God to ensure Moses' safety.

When Moses was old enough he went to live at the palace as the adopted son of the princess. He never forgot that he was an Israelite. He worshipped the true God, as his parents taught him.

When Moses was grown up, he saw an Egyptian beating an Israelite. He looked round to see that no one was watching and then killed the Egyptian and buried the body in the sand. Another day he saw two Israelite men fighting and tried to stop them. One of the men said to him, 'Do you mean to kill me, as you killed the Egyptian?'

Moses had been found out. Pharaoh was angry. Moses was so scared, he left Egypt and hid in the land of Midian on the other side of the Red Sea.

THINK: God knew all that Moses ever did. God knows what we do. The Scriptures teach us about God's salvation for sinners.

Moses got married in Midian and had two sons. He worked as a shepherd for his father-in-law. One day while he was looking after the sheep in the desert, he saw something very strange – a bush was on fire but was not being burnt up by the flames. When he went closer, God called out to him from the bush. 'Here I am,' said Moses.

'Don't come any closer,' God said. 'Take off your sandals for you are standing on holy ground.' Moses hid his face.

God said that he knew how unhappy his people were in Egypt.

'I have heard their cry. I know how they suffer. I am going to rescue them from the Egyptians. I will bring them to the lovely land of Canaan.'

'I am sending you to speak to Pharaoh and to lead my people out of Egypt.'

Moses was afraid of such a big task but God promised to help him.

THINK: When Moses asked God who he was, God said, 'Tell the people that "I AM" has sent you.' God's name, 'I AM', shows that he has always existed, that he is now and that he always will exist.

Moses was anxious about the task ahead.

'What if nobody believes that the LORD has spoken to me?'

'Throw your staff on the ground,' God said.

It immediately became a serpent.

'Catch it by the tail,' God commanded.

It became a staff again.

'This miracle and others will help them believe that God has appeared to you.'

'I am not a good speaker,' Moses objected.

'I have made your mouth,' said God. 'I will help you to speak.'

'Please send someone else,' pleaded Moses.

This made God angry.

'Your brother, Aaron, will work with you.' God said. 'He can speak well. Remember to take your staff with which you will work miracles.'

THINK: It is important to believe God's promises, and to trust in him. He always keeps his promises. If you are worried or anxious about anything trust in God to help you. The Bible tells us to cast our cares on the Lord for he cares for us.

Moses left Midian with his wife and family and headed back to Egypt. His brother, Aaron, met him in the desert. Moses told him all that the LORD had said. They met with the leaders of the Israelites and when they saw the miracles that God allowed Moses to do, they believed him. When they realised God was concerned about them, they bowed down and worshipped.

Moses and Aaron visited Pharaoh, and asked him to let the people go into the desert to make sacrifices to God. Pharaoh was furious.

'I will make their work even harder. They will have to gather the straw themselves and still make the same number of bricks.'

The people were overwhelmed with the extra work and complained to Moses. God promised that he would free them from slavery.

'I will take you as my own people. I will be your God. I will bring you to the land I promised to your forefathers.'

THINK: Slavery under Pharaoh was hard and distressing. Slavery to sin leads to misery and punishment. Christ Jesus is the great Saviour who delivers from sin by his death on the cross.

Pharaoh was hard and cruel. He refused to listen to Moses and Aaron. God told Moses what to do.

When Pharaoh went out to the river in the morning, Moses and Aaron met him and again asked him to let the people go to worship God in the desert. Pharaoh would not listen.

Aaron stretched out his staff over the river Nile. All the water was changed to blood. The fish died. The river smelled so bad, no one could drink the water for seven whole days. There was blood everywhere in Egypt.

Pharaoh was still stubborn. Each time Pharaoh refused, God sent another plague.

Swarms of frogs covered the land – into the houses (even the palace) – in the beds, the ovens, the cooking bowls.

'Get rid of the frogs,' said Pharaoh, 'and I will let you go.'

Moses prayed to the Lord and the Lord heard.

The frogs died and were swept up into heaps. When Pharaoh saw the frogs had gone, he changed his mind.

PRAY: Ask the Lord to help you to listen when he speaks to you and not ignore his Word, the Bible.

Another plague arrived. Annoying little gnats appeared from the dust. They covered the people and the animals.

Even Pharaoh's magicians said, 'This is the finger of God.' Still Pharaoh would not listen.

Next, swarms of flies were sent to plague the Egyptians. The Israelite people were not tormented by them at all.

'Sacrifice to your God here,' Pharaoh suggested.

'No,' said Moses, 'that would not be right. We must go for a three days' journey from here.'

'I will let you go,' said Pharaoh. 'Just get rid of these flies.'

Moses prayed to God.

The flies left Pharaoh and his people.

Deceitful Pharaoh changed his mind again and would not let the people go.

THINK: Pharoah hated God and his people. The Bible warns us that the wages of sin is death; but the good news is that the gift of God is eternal life through Jesus Christ.

The fifth plague that God sent to the Egyptians affected their animals. The horses, donkeys, camels, cattle, sheep and goats died. But the animals belonging to the Israelites were spared.

This had no effect on Pharaoh.

Then painful boils broke out on the skin of Egyptian people. Pharaoh still would not listen.

The Lord then sent heavy hailstones with thunder and lightning. It was the worst storm ever. It flattened the crops and stripped the trees of leaves. The only place it did not fall was the part where the Israelites lived.

Pharaoh showed some remorse. 'The Lord is right and I and my people are in the wrong,' he admitted. 'I will let you go.'

THINK: Pharaoh's actions did not match up to his words. He did not let the people go. We must be careful that our actions live up to our words. The Bible tells us to love not just with words, but in deed and in truth.

The LORD continued to send messages to Pharaoh. He wanted Moses and the Israelites to know that he was the powerful God.

'Swarms of locusts will come and eat any plant or leaf that has been left by the hail,' Moses told Pharaoh.

'Go away and worship your God,' ordered Pharaoh.

Moses made it clear that the women and children were to go too. Pharaoh would not agree to that.

So the locusts arrived making the ground black.

'I have sinned,' said Pharaoh. 'Pray to God to take the locusts away.'

But, as before, Pharaoh did not mean it. Intense darkness covered the land for three days. The Egyptians could not see each other or move from their homes. Still Pharaoh was stubborn.

THINK: Moses knew that it was vital that the women and children would also be able to go and worship God. Worship is not just for adults, but God wants little children to worship and praise him.

God told Moses, 'I will send one more plague on the Egyptians, then Pharaoh will let you go. At midnight I will go through Egypt. Every firstborn son in every family will die.'

This would be a terrible punishment.

That night every Egyptian household was affected. The eldest son died. Pharaoh's eldest son as well as the son of the prisoner in the dungeon. What grief there must have been in every Egyptian house.

However, this plague did not touch the Israelite people. God kept his people safe. He gave Moses special instructions for them to follow. Because God's people followed his commands they were delivered from the plague of death.

This was because they obeyed God's instructions to paint the doorposts and lintels of their house with the blood of a lamb.

PRAY: Ask the Lord God to help you to follow his commands. His ways are best. Thank him for his care for you.

God's instructions to the Israelites meant they were spared the suffering that the Egyptians had to face. They had been told to take the best lamb of the flock and kill it. The blood was then to be painted on the doorposts and lintel of the house. When the angel of death passed through Egypt, he would pass over the houses marked with blood.

The Israelites ate the roast lamb with bitter herbs and bread made without yeast. They were ordered to eat it in a hurry, ready for travelling – their cloaks tucked into their belts, sandals on their feet.

This meal was called the Passover Feast – remembering how the angel of death had passed over their houses. It was to be kept every year to remember what God had done for them.

God told the Israelites, 'When the children ask, "What does this ceremony mean to you?" Tell them, "It is the Passover sacrifice to the LORD who spared our lives when he struck the Egyptians."'

God had kept his promise to his people. They bowed down to worship him.

THINK: The blood on the doorposts reminds us of another great escape. Jesus Christ shed his blood on the cross at Calvary so that his people would escape eternal death. Jesus ate the Passover Feast with his disciples the night before he died on the cross.

Pharaoh changed his mind at last. 'Go and serve the LORD. Take your flocks and herds with you.'

The Egyptians were desperate to get rid of the Israelite people.

God's people, the Israelites, started out on their journey from slavery in Egypt heading for the promised land of Canaan. They took their dough and their kneading bowls wrapped up in cloth. They asked the Egyptians to give them silver and gold and clothing and they gladly did so.

Six hundred thousand men left Egypt that night as well as women and children. They took their sheep and cattle too. God guided them with a pillar of cloud during the day and a pillar of fire at night-time.

THINK: God rescued his people from slavery in Egypt. He rescues his people today from slavery to sin, through his Son, the Lord Jesus Christ. All who trust in him are freed from slavery to sin.

Once the Israelite slaves were gone, Pharaoh had second thoughts. Who would do all the hard work now? Pharaoh's soldiers chased after them. When the Israelites reached the Red Sea they felt trapped – sea in front and soldiers behind. They complained to Moses. 'You have taken us here to die in the desert.'

'Do not be afraid,' Moses encouraged. 'Stand firm and see the salvation of the LORD.'

The angel of the LORD went behind them. The pillar of cloud moved behind them too – keeping the Egyptians in darkness. God told Moses to hold out his staff over the Red Sea. God drove the sea back by a strong east wind. Moses led the people across on dry ground. The Egyptian soldiers tried to follow, but their chariot wheels stuck. God told Moses to stretch out his hand again over the sea, drowning the Egyptian army.

THINK: When we feel afraid, we should remember that our great and powerful God is always with us. If God is for us, who can be against us?

After walking for three days the people were desperate for water. At last they found some at Marah but it was so bitter it was undrinkable.

The people grumbled to Moses, 'What are we going to drink?'

Moses cried out in prayer to the LORD. God showed him a piece of wood. Moses threw the wood into the water and the water became sweet and drinkable.

'If you listen to me and obey my words,' God told them, 'I will look after you for I am the LORD who heals you.'

When they came to Elim they camped there near springs of water and palm trees.

THINK: God is the same today. He wants us to listen to his Word and obey him. God cares for all our physical needs. Every good gift comes from him. But our greatest need is Salvation. We must praise God for giving us his one and only Son, the Lord Jesus, to save lost sinners.

Again the people complained. 'We used to have plenty to eat in Egypt. Now we are so hungry.'

God heard them and provided. That evening the camp was covered with birds called quails. They had plenty of meat to eat. God provided bread too. In the morning the ground was covered with little white seeds called manna.

Each family collected what they needed for the day. When the sun grew hot, it melted away. On the sixth day of the week, they collected twice as much, some to use on the Sabbath day. God did not send manna on the Sabbath.

God provided this food during all the years that the Israelites travelled in the desert.

THINK: Jesus said that he is the Bread of Life sent from heaven by God. Only Jesus can fully satisfy a longing heart.

The Israelites still grumbled. 'There is no water to drink here,' they complained. 'Why did you bring us out of Egypt to die of thirst?'

Moses cried to God for help. God told Moses what to do. 'Take your rod. Speak to that rock and it will yield water for you.'

Moses stood in front of the rock as the people watched. He spoke angrily to the people and hit the rock. Water came rushing out.

God provided for his people but he was displeased that Moses had not obeyed him exactly. As a punishment God did not allow Moses to enter the Promised Land. He only saw it from a distance.

THINK: God provided refreshment for the people from the rock. For us he provides living water to refresh our souls from the Lord Jesus Christ 'If any one thirsts,' said Jesus, 'let him come to me and drink.'

63. Amalekites Defeated - Exodus 17

The Amalekites attacked the Israelites at Rephidim. Moses said to his assistant, Joshua, 'Choose some men and go out to fight the Amalekites.'

Moses stood on the top of a nearby hill with the staff of God in his hands. Aaron and Hur went with him.

Joshua and his army fought the Amalekites. As long as Moses kept his hands up, the Israelites were winning. But if he let his hands fall down, the Amalekites would win. When Moses' hands grew tired, he sat on a big stone. Aaron and Hur stood on each side of him and held his hands up steady until sunset. So Joshua and his army had the victory.

'Be sure to tell Joshua what happened,' God told Moses. Moses built an altar there and called it 'The LORD is my Banner.'

THINK: God's people are in a battle against sin and the evil one, Satan. But through the Lord God they have the victory.

Jethro, the priest of Midian, Moses' father-in-law, heard about what God had done for Moses and his people. He went to visit Moses in the desert. He was delighted to hear from Moses all the good things that God had done, rescuing them from the Egyptians.

He saw how hard Moses had to work, settling disputes and making judgements from morning till night. He gave him some good advice. 'You will wear yourself out. The work is too heavy. You cannot handle it alone. Get others to help you. Choose able, truthful men and train them to make decisions. When a difficult case comes up, you can deal with that.'

Moses acted on this good advice, and appointed officials to deal with the easier cases. Moses' workload became less. He only dealt with the difficult decisions.

THINK: Moses showed respect to his father-in-law by taking his advice. God wants us to show respect to our parents too. One of his commandments is to honour our father and mother.

Three months after they left Egypt, Moses and the people reached the Desert of Sinai. They set up camp at the foot of Mount Sinai.

God spoke to Moses from the mountain, 'I am going to allow the people to hear my voice,' said God, 'so that they will trust you.'

The people gathered at the foot of the mountain. 'Be careful not to touch the mountain at all. If you do, you will die.'

Three days later, thick cloud covered the mountain. Thunder rolled and lightning flashed. A very loud trumpet sounded out. Everyone trembled with fear.

The LORD descended on Mount Sinai in fire, covering it with smoke.

God called Moses to the top of the mountain. The people remained at a distance, while Moses went into the thick darkness where God was.

THINK: God is awesome, worthy of worship and to be feared. His glory is above the heavens yet he is gracious and merciful to us and shows us such care and love.

God spoke to Moses on Mount Sinai and gave the Ten Commandments for his people to obey. The first four were about God and how he was to be worshipped.

'You shall not worship any God but me. You shall not make any idol. You shall not speak God's name in vain. Keep the Sabbath day holy.'

Six commandments then told how the people were to treat others.

'Honour your father and mother. Do not murder. Do not commit adultery. Do not steal. Do not bear false witness. Do not covet what belongs to someone else.'

God gave Moses many detailed laws about how to live in the family and community, how to stay healthy, how to worship God. Moses wrote them down. He was on Mount Sinai for forty days and nights. God gave him two tablets of stone with the Ten Commandments written on them by the finger of God.

THINK: The only man who could keep this law perfectly was Jesus Christ, the Son of God who became man. He was completely without sin.

The people grew impatient waiting for Moses to come back down the mountain.

'We don't know what's happened to Moses. Make us an idol to worship,' they asked Aaron.

Sadly he agreed. They collected gold earrings, melted them together and made a golden calf. They worshipped this calf and made sacrifices to it.

When Moses came down the mountain and saw the idol and the people dancing around, he became very angry. He threw the two tablets of stone to the ground breaking them in pieces. He smashed the golden calf into powder, mixed it with water and made the people drink it. They were punished severely for their sin.

Moses went back to the LORD and prayed for forgiveness.

The LORD graciously called Moses to Mount Sinai and wrote the Ten Commandments on two other tablets of stone.

THINK: God's second commandment forbids the worshipping of idols. God is a Spirit and the Bible tells us to worship him in spirit and truth, from the heart.

The journey to the Promised Land was long and hard. The people grew impatient and grumbled against God and against Moses.

'Why did you bring us out of Egypt to die in the desert?' they moaned.

God sent poisonous snakes into the camp. Many of the rebellious Israelites were bitten and died.

'We have sinned against God,' the rest confessed to Moses. 'Please pray that God would take the snakes away.'

God told Moses to make a brass snake and set it up on a pole in the camp. Anyone who had been bitten just had to look at the brass snake and they would be cured.

THINK: Jesus mentioned this story and compared himself to that brass snake. Anyone who looks to Jesus in faith will be cured of the disease of sin.

God gave Moses special instructions about erecting a place where he could be worshipped in the camp. A tent, or tabernacle, was made of goats' hair lined with blue, purple and scarlet linen.

Inside the most Holy Place was placed a beautiful box of acacia wood covered in gold and decorated with two golden cherubim. The tablets containing the ten commandments were placed in this box.

Two men, Bezaleal and Aholiab, were given special skill and knowledge by God to be in charge of this amazing work.

Instructions were given by God through Moses to make a table, dishes and bowls, a lampstand, an altar for sacrifices, and a big basin for washing as well.

This place for worship was carried from camp to camp on their wanderings in the desert.

THINK: We can worship God anywhere – at home, on the bus, in school. We give him the glory due to him by obeying his Word and trusting in him through the Lord Jesus.

The Levites, (the family of Levi, one of Jacob's sons) were the priests in charge of worship in the tabernacle. God told Moses how he, the LORD God, ought to be worshipped. Sacrifices of specially chosen animals were to be made on the altar, to say thank you to God or sorry for sins committed.

Feasts and holy days were times of joyful thanks to God.

The most important priest was the High Priest. He had special clothes – a tunic with a sash, a breastplate, an ephod (a vest with shoulder straps), a robe and a turban. Only the High Priest could enter the Most Holy Place in the tabernacle once a year to offer a special sacrifice to God.

THINK: These offerings were given to God by his people until the Lord Jesus made the perfect offering for sin on the cross once for all.

2. Joshua, Judges, and the Kings

Books of the Bible:

Numbers, Deuteronomy, Joshua, Judges, Ruth,
1st and 2nd Samuel, 1st and 2nd Kings,
1st and 2nd Chronicles, Psalms, Jeremiah.

What you will read about:

The Promised Land, Joshua, Crossing
the Jordan, Battles, Victories and
Defeats, Ehud and Eglon, Deborah and
Barak, Jael and Sisera, Gideon, Samson,
Ruth, Samuel, Saul, David, Solomon,
Elijah, Elisha, The Divided Kingdom.

Moses sent twelve men to spy out the Promised Land. They returned with a huge bunch of grapes. It was so big, two men had to carry it between them on a large pole. They all said the land was prosperous. But ten of the men said that the people there were too strong for them to conquer. The Israelites became afraid.

Joshua and Caleb did not agree with the other spies, however. 'The land is very good,' they said. 'Do not be afraid. The LORD is with us.'

Many of the people doubted God. God did not allow these people to see the Promised Land. For forty years they wandered in the wilderness. Only Joshua and Caleb and those under twenty at that time lived to enter the Promised Land. The rest died in the wilderness.

THINK: God has promised to guide all who trust in him. Do not rely on your own understanding; acknowledge him in everything and he will direct you.

Joshua became the leader of the Israelites after the death of Moses. God encouraged him at the start of his great task with these words, 'Be strong and of good courage. Do not be afraid, do not be dismayed, for the LORD your God is with you wherever you go.'

Joshua's job was to lead the people right into the Promised Land of Canaan. 'I will give you this land,' God assured him. 'I will be with you and I will not fail you.'

Joshua obeyed God immediately. He gave orders to the officers. 'Tell everyone to get ready. We will soon cross over the River Jordan to the land of Canaan.'

The people did as he said.

THINK: When you are afraid, think of God's message to Joshua and to you. 'Do not be afraid for I am with you.'

73. Rahab Hides the Spies - Joshua 2

Joshua sent two men to spy on the city of Jericho. They were spotted but a woman called Rahab hid them under stalks of flax on the flat roof of her home. When the soldiers came searching, she sent them away to look elsewhere.

Rahab's house was on the town wall. She helped the spies escape down a scarlet rope from her window to the ground.

'When we come back to take the city,' the spies told her, 'tie this scarlet rope in the window as a sign. All the people in the house with you will be safe.'

'The LORD has given us this land,' the spies told Joshua.

THINK: Rahab was an ancestor of the Lord Jesus Christ. God's grace reaches out to all nations and all types of people.

Joshua and the people got up early in the morning. God told Joshua what to do. Joshua passed on the orders to the people.

As soon as the priests' feet stepped into the river Jordan, the water stopped flowing. The priests stood in the middle of the dry riverbed. The people walked across safely into the land of Canaan. God's wonderful power was at work.

Joshua built a pillar of twelve stones on the riverbed where the priests had stood. He ordered twelve men to take a stone each and carry them to Gilgal, the next campsite. There they built another pillar.

Joshua told the people, 'When your children ask what these stones mean, you will tell them how God stopped the River Jordan flowing to allow us to pass over safely.' It is good to remember how good God is to us.

THINK: God's Word reminds us of his goodness to us. We can pass on to others the good news that God has sent his Son to save sinners like us.

God told Joshua how he must capture the city of Jericho. Joshua and the people obeyed.

For six days the people marched once each day, round the walls of the city.

In front were the armed guards, seven priests each blowing a trumpet, then priests carrying the Ark of Covenant. Then came more soldiers.

No fighting, just marching round.

On the seventh day they marched round not just once, but seven times.

On the seventh time Joshua told the people, 'Shout, for God has given you the city.'

When the people shouted, and the trumpets blew, the walls of Jericho fell down flat.

The Israelites went straight into the city and destroyed it.

Joshua did not forget Rahab and her kindness to the spies. He sent the two men to her house and she and her family were saved alive.

THINK: Joshua and his men listened to God and obeyed him. God gave the victory. The glory was all his.

All the silver and gold and valuable things in Jericho belonged to the LORD. One man, Achan, stole some silver and gold and clothes for himself. He hid them in the ground under his tent. God, who sees everything, knew what he had done.

Achan's sin brought trouble to the whole nation. They thought they would easily take the next city, Ai, but the men of Ai won the battle and chased them away.

Joshua was upset and asked God why they had been defeated. God told him that someone in the camp had sinned by stealing what belonged to God.

Joshua rose early in the morning and God guided him to find out that Achan was the man in the camp who had committed this sin. The silver and gold and a beautiful robe were recovered from under Achan's tent.

Achan was severely punished. The people threw stones at him until he died. The LORD told Joshua to go again to capture Ai. This time they were successful.

THINK: God hates sin. He has to punish it. God sent his Son into the world to take the punishment for the sins of those who trust in him.

When the land of Canaan was divided up among the tribes of Israel, the tribe of Levi (the Levites) did not receive a share. They were given the special task of being God's holy priests, taking care of the sacrifices and other duties connected to the worship of God. They would have no time to plough the land or harvest crops.

The other tribes agreed to provide them with a share of their crops. The Levites were given cities to live in throughout the land and pasture land for their flocks and herds. They were to dedicate their lives to the work of the LORD. The LORD God was their inheritance.

THINK: Many people today work for God in churches or in missions in foreign lands. Christians should support them in their special work by giving money and by praying.

After the land was divided up, Joshua set apart special cities to be cities of refuge, just as the LORD had instructed Moses.

If anyone killed a person accidentally, he could run to one of these cities where he would be safe from an attack from a relative seeking revenge. So long as he stayed in the city he would be safe. The cities chosen were well spread out so that one of them was easily reached from any part of the country. The cities were Kedesh, Shechem, and Hebron in the hill country on the west of the Jordan, and Bezar, Ramoth and Golan on the east side of the Jordan.

THINK: The Lord Jesus is a refuge for sinners if we run to him by faith. God is our refuge and strength.

79. God's Promise Fulfilled - Joshua 8 — 24

Joshua built an altar to the LORD on Mount Ebal. There the people worshipped the LORD. Joshua read out the whole law of God to the people. God helped them to defeat the whole land of Canaan. Then there was peace throughout the land. God's promise was fulfilled.

Joshua had another important task – to share out the land so that each of the Israelite tribes had its own part to live in.

When Joshua grew old he called the chief men of Israel together and gave them good advice. 'You must serve the LORD alone,' he urged them. 'Choose today whom you will serve, but as for me and my family, we will serve the LORD.'

The people replied, 'We will serve the LORD our God and obey him.'

THINK: The most important choice we can make is to serve God. We should pray that God would make us willing to make this choice.

The people followed God while Joshua was alive, but the next generation forgot what God had done for them. They started to worship false gods like Baal and their children were not taught about the one true God who had brought them out of slavery in Egypt.

This made God angry. God allowed their enemies to overpower them, causing them great distress. God in his mercy, sent them leaders called judges who guided them in God's ways for a time. When the judges died, the people went back to their old ways.

Time and again the people of Israel did evil in God's eyes. Their enemies caused them great distress and they cried out for help. God never stopped loving them and sent another man to help them.

THINK: God's mercy to sinners is so great that he sent his Son into the world to die so that the sins of his people would be forgiven.

King Eglon of Moab attacked Israel and ruled over the land for eighteen years. The Israelites cried out to God and this time he gave them a deliverer called Ehud. He was chosen to travel to Moab to deliver the annual tax money to Eglon. He hid in his clothing a double-edged dagger.

On the return journey, he sent his companions ahead and returned to see King Eglon (who was a very fat man). 'I have a secret message for you,' he told Eglon. Eglon told all his servants to leave the room. 'It is a message from God.'

Eglon stood up to receive the message. Ehud reached with his left hand for the hidden dagger and plunged it into the king's fat belly, killing him. Ehud escaped back to Israel and mustered an army which conquered the Moabite army.

Israel lived at peace then for the next eighty years.

THINK: When the people of Israel prayed for help, God heard them and delivered them from the enemy in a most unusual way. When we are in trouble we can pray to the same God who promises to help in time of need.

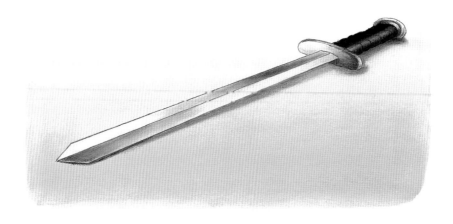

After Ehud died, the people of Israel forgot about God. So God let them be conquered by King Jabin. For twenty years he made their lives miserable. At last they cried out to God for help.

In Israel at that time there was a wise woman called Deborah. She called on Barak to gather together a large army, to fight King Jabin's army and his general Sisera.

'I'll go', Barak said, 'but only if you go with me.'

Deborah agreed. Ten thousand men volunteered and Deborah went with them. She encouraged Barak and the soldiers. 'The LORD is leading us. He has delivered Sisera into your hand.'

The enemy soldiers were thrown into a panic and Barak and his men chased them away. General Sisera escaped.

THINK: God is wise in everything he does. He allowed his people to suffer under the enemy king. At last they cried out for help again. Ask God to help you never to forget him.

Sisera, the general of King Jabin's army crept away from the battle scene, and hid in a tent belonging to a woman called Jael. He thought he was safe there.

He lay down and she covered him with a blanket.

'Please give me some water,' he asked. 'I am very thirsty.'

So she gave him some milk.

Sisera went off to sleep. Jael took a sharp tent peg and a hammer and quietly crept up and hammered the peg through his head, killing him.

When Barak came looking for his enemy, Jael showed him what she had done. Israel had peace again for forty years, but they still did evil in God's sight and began to worship false gods. However, God did not abandon them.

THINK: God is so patient with his rebellious people. Jesus was patient with his followers even when they turned from him at the time of his death.

Gideon lived in Israel during troubled times. Enemies from the land of Midian stole sheep and cattle, and the crops. The people were frightened. They had to escape to the mountains and live in caves.

They cried out to God in prayer for help. God did not answer their prayers straight away. He knew what they needed. God sent a prophet to the people with a message from himself.

'I saved you from the Egyptians and brought you to this land. I am the LORD your God. But you have not obeyed my voice.'

This was why Gideon and his people were in trouble.

But God had a plan to help them. God was in control.

THINK: God sent a prophet to the people with a message. Jesus is the great prophet that God sent to us with the message of salvation.

85. God Chooses Gideon – Judges 6

One day Gideon was threshing some wheat. He hid in a wine press so that the Midianite soldiers would not see him and steal his food. An angel of God came and sat down under an oak tree. Gideon did not know who this stranger was.

'God has chosen you to save your country from the enemy,' the angel said.

Gideon was so surprised. 'How can I save Israel? I am the least important in my family and my family is not great.'

'Surely I will be with you,' the LORD said. 'You shall defeat the Midianites.'

'Please do not go away,' Gideon said to the angel. 'Wait there until I make some food for you.'

The angel graciously waited. Gideon fetched bread and meat in a basket and a pot of broth.

'Put the food on this rock,' the angel told Gideon, 'And then pour out the broth.'

The angel touched the food with the end of his stick. Fire rose up out of the rock and burnt up the food completely. Then the angel disappeared.

Gideon now knew that he had been talking to an angel of God.

'Do not be afraid,' God said to him.

Gideon built an altar so that he could worship God there.

THINK: When Gideon was afraid, God assured him that he would be with him. Jesus promised his disciples that he would be with them always.

Gideon worshipped the one true God. God instructed him to tear down the places where the people worshipped the false god, Baal. This was a good thing to do but it was unpopular with the people.

Gideon had been told that he would save his people from the Midianites. But he was unsure. He asked God to do something special for him. He took a sheep's fleece and put it on the ground one night.

Gideon asked God to make the fleece wet with dew but to leave the ground round it dry. If that happened, he would know that he was God's chosen man. God granted Gideon's request. Gideon squeezed out a whole bowlful of water from the fleece. But he still had doubts and wanted yet another sign.

'Do not be angry with me. Please give me another sign,' he asked God. 'Let the fleece be dry and the ground wet with dew.'

When Gideon checked the fleece in the morning, God had again answered his prayer. Gideon was now sure that he would be the leader of Israel to save them from the enemy.

THINK: Gideon asked for special guidance from God. We have the most wonderful guidance – God's very own inspired, inerrant Word.

Gideon had a huge army of 32,000 soldiers. God said to Gideon, 'Your army is too big. If you win the battle you will think that you have done it in your own strength.'

Gideon said to the soldiers, 'If any of you are afraid and want to go home, just go.' So 22,000 men went home. Gideon's army of 10,000 men was still too big.

God said to Gideon, 'Take the men down to the river to drink. I will show you which ones to keep.' Many of the men went down on their knees and put their mouths right into the water to drink. God told Gideon to send these men home.

There were only 300 men who drank by scooping up the water in their hands. God told Gideon to keep them as his soldiers. That night God told Gideon to go down secretly to the enemy camp. He took a friend with him. Down they crept in the darkness. They overheard a man in his tent telling about a strange dream. 'A loaf of bread tumbled down into the camp and knocked over one of the tents. I wonder what it means.'

'I know what it means,' his friend replied. 'God is going to help Gideon to defeat us.'

Gideon was so encouraged when he overheard this conversation. He worshipped the LORD.

THINK: We should remember that without God we can do nothing, but with God all things are possible.

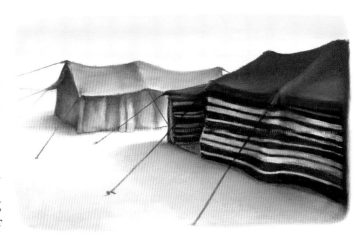

Gideon got ready for battle. He divided his men into three groups. Each group was to approach the enemy from a different direction.

Every soldier had a trumpet and a lamp covered with a jug to hide the light. Gideon told them to watch him closely and follow his instructions.

In the middle of the night, Gideon and his army marched towards the enemy camp, waiting for Gideon's sign. Suddenly Gideon blew his trumpet. They all blew their trumpets too. They smashed the jugs so that the lamps shone brightly. They shouted as loudly as they could, 'The sword of the LORD and of Gideon!'

The enemy soldiers were terrified when they heard the noise and saw the lights. They ran to and fro and started fighting with each other. Then they ran off in panic. Gideon and his men chased them right out of the land. Gideon had saved his people as God had promised.

After the victory the people asked Gideon to be their king.

'No,' replied Gideon. 'The LORD will rule over you.'

THINK: The Lord Jesus Christ is our great king, ruling over us wisely, defending us from our enemies – sin and Satan.

89. God our Peace - Judges 6

God used Gideon, the least important in his family, to win a great victory for the nation.

The angel of God appeared to him and assured him of his peace. Gideon called the place, 'The LORD is Peace'.

God asks us to pray about everything and give thanks.

Those who love the LORD God and trust in him are promised this gift of peace. Even if life is full of trouble and worry, God's own peace can calm our hearts. This peace is only possible through the Lord Jesus who took our punishment and gained our salvation from sin. When we trust him in faith, we have peace with God.

THINK: Jesus gave a special message to his disciples, as he promised that the Holy Spirit would be with them. 'Peace I leave with you; my peace I give you. Not as the world gives do I give to you; Let not your hearts be troubled, neither let them be afraid,' John 14: 27.

Time and again the Israelites rebelled against God. God allowed their enemies, the Philistines, to conquer the land and rule over them for forty years.

Manoah and his wife had no children. One day an angel of the LORD appeared to Manoah's wife and told her she would soon have a son. He gave her special instructions about his upbringing.

She rushed to tell her husband the news. Manoah prayed to God, 'Come again to teach us how to bring up the boy.'

The angel of the LORD appeared to them both, but only after he had ascended in the flame of their burning offering did Manoah realise that their visitor was indeed the angel of the LORD.

When the baby boy, Samson, was born, his parents did as the angel instructed. He was dedicated to God – as a Nazirite he never had his hair cut nor drank strong drink.

The LORD blessed him as he grew up.

THINK: God spoke to Manoah and his wife by an angel. He speaks to us today through his Word, the Bible. The Bible gives guidance on the way we should live.

Samson grew up to be very strong. He fell in love with a Philistine woman and wanted to marry her. On the way to visit her, he was attacked by a lion. With God's help he killed it with his bare hands. Some time later when he travelled the road again to go to get married, he saw that bees had made honey inside the body of the dead lion. He scooped it out and ate it and gave some to his parents.

At his wedding Samson told a riddle. 'Out of the eater, something to eat; out of the strong, something sweet.' If the Philistine guests couldn't solve the riddle in seven days, they had to give Samson thirty sets of clothes. But if they did solve it, Samson had to give them thirty sets of clothes.

Samson's new wife cried until he explained the riddle. She then told the others and they won the challenge. Samson had been betrayed. He was so angry, he killed thirty men and took their clothes for the Philistines. Samson went back to his father's house and his wife married someone else.

THINK: Jesus knew what it was like to be betrayed by a friend, when Judas sold him to the authorities, but he did not become angry.

Samson was so angry that his wife had married someone else. Her family would not let him see her. He decided to take revenge on the Philistines. He caught 300 foxes and tied them in pairs by their tails, fastened torches to them and let them loose in the corn fields. The cornfields, vineyards and olive groves belonging to the Philistines were all burnt up.

Men from Judah captured Samson to hand him over to the Philistines because they were afraid that war would break out. Samson was so strong he easily broke the ropes tying him up. He killed 1,000 men with the jaw-bone of an ass.

Samson was the leader of the Israelites for twenty years.

THINK: Samson used his exceptional strength in surprising ways. Paul knew that his strength was only in the Lord God. He knew this strength, even when he was physically weak. God gives us our strength. We should be thankful for what God enables us to do.

Samson fell in love with a woman called Delilah. The Philistines asked her to discover the secret of his strength. Three times Samson lied to her but finally she persuaded him to tell her the truth. If his hair was cut he would become as weak as any man.

That night when Samson slept in her lap, a man shaved off Samson's long hair. Samson's vow to the LORD had been broken. God's strength left him. The Philistines captured him, gouged out his eyes and put him in prison.

In prison his hair grew again and one day he was brought up to the temple so all could see him and be entertained. Samson stood beside the temple pillars and leant on them. Then he prayed to God for strength so that he could get revenge on the Philistines. The LORD gave him strength and he pushed the two pillars down, making the temple collapse. Samson died with the Philistines. He killed more people at his death than he had during his lifetime.

THINK: Samson was a deliverer for the people of Israel. Our great deliverer is the Lord Jesus Christ, who saves us from all our sins.

A family from Bethlehem in Israel came to live in Moab because there was a famine in their land. Elimelech and Naomi came with their two sons, Mahlon and Chilion, to live more comfortably in Moab. They worshipped the true God. Sadly, Elimelech died in Moab. When Mahlon and Chilion grew up they married two local girls – Ruth and Orpah.

Ruth and Orpah lived in the land of Moab. Their families did not worship God. They worshipped idols.

Ruth stopped worshipping idols and began to trust in the true God and to worship him. Later, more sorrow came to the family. Both Mahlon and Chilion died. Naomi and Orpah and Ruth were now widows with no men to support them or provide for them. Naomi was many miles away from her friends in Israel. What would she do?

THINK: Many sad events occur in our lives. We can tell God all about our sadness. He cares and comforts.

One day Naomi said to Ruth and Orpah, 'I must go back to Bethlehem. I have heard there is plenty food there now.'

Ruth and Orpah set off with her.

After some distance Naomi said, 'Girls, you have come far enough. Go back to your own people now.'

'We do not want to leave you,' they both said.

But eventually Orpah changed her mind and returned to her home in Moab.

But Ruth would not go. She said to Naomi, 'Please do not tell me to leave you. I will go wherever you go. I will live where you live. Your people will be my people, and your God will be my God.'

Ruth chose to follow God and to be with God's people.

Ruth and Naomi arrived in Bethlehem at harvest time.

THINK: The God of the Bible is the only true God. Many people worship false gods. This is sinful. The Lord God is the only one to worship.

Poor people like Ruth were allowed to gather up the grain that had been dropped or left behind in the fields. Ruth asked Naomi if she could go and do this one day. She hoped to bring home some barley to make bread. Naomi encouraged her to go.

God guided her to a field belonging to Boaz. Boaz noticed Ruth and asked who she was. He found out that she was Naomi's daughter-in-law. He went to speak to Ruth and was very kind to her. 'Do not go to any other field to glean,' he said. 'Stay beside my girls. When you are thirsty, help yourself to our water. I have heard how kind you have been to Naomi and how you have come to trust in the Lord God.'

Boaz quietly told his men, 'Let Ruth glean anywhere in the field. Drop some handfuls of barley specially for her to gather.'

At the end of the day, Ruth carried home a large basket full of grain.

Naomi was delighted.

THINK: God showed his care for Ruth by providing for her needs. God shows his care for us by providing food, clothing, homes, family, but especially salvation through Christ Jesus.

Naomi spoke to Ruth one day, 'I would love to see you happily married again. Mahlon's closest relative should, by our law, marry you and buy back or redeem our land. I believe Boaz would help.' Boaz was a relative of Naomi's late husband.

Naomi told Ruth what to do. After dark she went to where Boaz was resting to ask him privately to redeem or buy back the family land and be a kinsman-redeemer for her.

'I would gladly help you,' he said, 'but there is a closer relative I must ask first.' Ruth went home with a big gift of barley for Naomi.

That morning Boaz met with the relative at the town gate. He did not wish to marry Ruth so Boaz told the people gathered there, 'I now have the right to buy the land that belonged to Elimelech and to marry Ruth.'

Boaz and Ruth were soon married and God gave them the gift of a baby son, Obed. Naomi was again full of joy.

THINK: Joy is a gift of God that we can have through the Lord Jesus. The good news of the gospel gives us great joy.

Ruth's baby was important. He became the grandfather of the great king David, who wrote most of the lovely Psalms in the Bible.

But the most important descendant of Boaz and Ruth was the Lord Jesus Christ, who was born in Bethlehem many years later.

Boaz was a redeemer for Ruth. Jesus Christ is the Redeemer for his people. His people are redeemed from a life of sin and misery. The price he paid was not money but his own precious blood. Jesus Christ gave his life as a redemption payment, when he died on the cross.

PRAY: Thank the Lord for sending his Son into this world to be the Redeemer for those who trust in him.

Hannah and her husband, Elkanah, lived in the town of Ramah in Israel.

In those days some good men had more than one wife. People in Israel at that time were living just like people who did not believe in God – they should have known better.

Elkanah had another wife called Peninnah who had several children. Hannah was sad that she did not have a child. She longed to have a baby son.

Every year Elkanah took his family to the Tabernacle to worship God. At that time he gave gifts to all the family, but Hannah received a special gift because he loved her best of all. However, this did not make up for the fact that Hannah did not have a baby. Peninnah mocked her. This made Hannah miserable. She could not eat her food and cried a great deal. Not even Elkanah could comfort her.

'Why are you so sad?' he asked. 'Am I not better to you than ten sons?'

Hannah knew that the only one who could help her was the LORD God.

THINK: We can worship God anywhere, and anytime, but it is good to go to God's house regularly to worship him, along with other people.

One day in Shiloh, Hannah made her way alone to the Temple of the LORD. She felt so sad. She wept and prayed and told all her problems to the LORD.

As she prayed, she promised God, 'If you will remember me and give me a baby boy, I will give him back to work for you all his life.'

Eli the priest sat watching Hannah. He noticed her lips moving soundlessly. He thought she looked strange. Eli thought she was drunk. 'How long are you going to be drunk? Stop drinking so much wine!' he said to Hannah.

Hannah replied, 'I have not been drinking wine at all. I am in great distress and have been telling the LORD all about it.'

Eli realised his mistake and said, 'Go in peace and may the LORD give you what you have asked for.'

Hannah believed that God would answer her prayer and went back home very happy.

THINK: God loves to hear his people praying to him. We can tell him about any concern we have.

Hannah had a baby son of her own. She was very happy. God had answered her prayer. She gave him the special name 'Samuel' which means 'asked of God'. Hannah remembered how she had prayed to God for this baby.

The next time Elkanah went to Shiloh to worship the LORD, Hannah stayed at home with young Samuel. 'I will take him to Shiloh when he is a little older. Then I will give him to the LORD and he will stay there always,' she explained.

So when Samuel was old enough, Hannah took him to the house of the LORD in Shiloh.

She reminded Eli the priest of their last meeting.

'I am the woman you saw praying here. I prayed for this child. I am now keeping my promise and returning the child to work for the LORD.'

Samuel stayed in the Tabernacle from that day – helping Eli with lots of tasks. Hannah and Elkanah visited him every year. Each time Hannah brought him a new coat which she had made herself.

Hannah praised God for his goodness and kindness to her. 'There is no one so great as God,' she said. 'He has made the whole world and rules over everyone.'

THINK: When God answers prayer, it should lead us to praise him too. God is great and deserves our praise.

Samuel worked hard for God in the Tabernacle. He helped Eli the priest and worshipped God every day.

One evening Eli, who was nearly blind, went to bed as usual. Young Samuel also went to bed. As he lay there he heard a voice calling his name.

'Samuel.'

'Eli must be wanting me,' he thought.

'Here I am,' he answered as he ran through to Eli. 'You were calling me.'

'I did not call you,' replied Eli. 'Go back to bed.'

Again he heard someone calling, 'Samuel.'

Again Samuel got up and went to Eli.

'Here I am,' he said. 'You did call me.'

'I did not,' said Eli. 'Lie down again.'

God was really calling Samuel, but he did not realise it.

THINK: God spoke to the little boy, Samuel. He still speaks to little children through his Word, the Bible. Be sure to listen to his message.

When Samuel went through to Eli for the third time, Eli knew that the voice Samuel was hearing was God's voice. He told him what to do. When God spoke again to Samuel, he knew to reply, 'Speak, for your servant is listening.'

God told Samuel that Eli's sons were very wicked and because Eli did not punish them, the whole family would be punished.

Samuel lay in bed thinking about what had happened. In the morning he got up to open the doors to the House of the LORD.

He was afraid to tell Eli what God had told him, but Eli asked him what God's message was.

'Don't hide anything from me,' he said.

After Samuel told him, Eli humbly said, 'He is the LORD; let him do what seems best to him.'

God was with Samuel as he grew up, and guided him. God will guide you also through his Holy Word.

THINK: Samuel grew up to be a great prophet, speaking God's words. Jesus is the greatest prophet, speaking God's truth to us.

Israel was in trouble. The Philistines had defeated them and had even captured the Ark of the Covenant.

The people were sad because it seemed as if God had abandoned them. Samuel told them, 'If you are serious about returning to the LORD, destroy all the idols and false gods that you have been worshipping. I will pray to the LORD for you.'

The people gathered with Samuel. They went without food to show that they were truly sorry for their sins. The Philistines decided to advance with a great army against them. The Israelites were very afraid. 'Pray to God to save us,' they urged Samuel.

Samuel offered a sacrifice to the LORD and prayed for help. A huge thunderstorm alarmed and confused the Philistines so much, that the Israelites were able to chase them away. Samuel erected a monument to remind Israel that God had helped them.

THINK: When we have problems and worries, the first thing to do is to pray to God about them like Samuel did.

Samuel was wise but his sons were not. They were greedy and accepted bribes. The people were not happy. 'Give us a king like other countries,' they begged.

Samuel was upset, but God told him to go ahead. 'The people are not rejecting you, they are rejecting me,' said God.

God, the LORD, is the true king of his people. God is the king of all the earth.

Saul, a handsome young man, was sent to search for some missing donkeys. He and his servant had no success and decided to ask for help from Samuel.

When Samuel saw Saul coming towards him, the LORD said, 'That is the man who will be the first king of Israel.'

Saul and Samuel ate a meal together and talked well into the night. Before Saul left the next morning, Samuel took a flask of oil and poured it on Saul's head. This was the sign that Saul was to be the king.

THINK: Wisdom is a gift from God. James 1:5 tells us that we should ask God for it. Psalm 111:10 tells us that the beginning of wisdom is when we trust and obey God.

Saul was a successful and powerful king at first but then things changed. Saul did not carry out all of God's commands. He disobeyed him, choosing to please the people rather than God.

Samuel had to tell him that God was displeased with him, and had rejected him as king. 'God has found another man to be king,' he told him, 'a man after his own heart.'

Again and again Saul went his own way, disobeying God's commands. When his army defeated the Amalekites, God told him to take no plunder at all; but Saul took the best of the sheep and cattle. Samuel heard the noise of the animals and challenged Saul.

'I kept these to sacrifice to God,' he said.

'To obey God is better than to sacrifice,' Samuel told him.

THINK: God wants us to obey his commands which he has shown us in his Word. We fail to do this so often, but the Lord Jesus Christ is the perfect example of obedience.

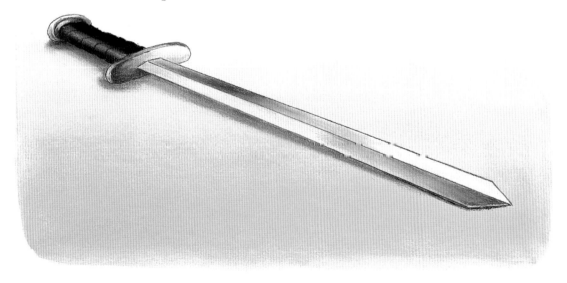

David was the youngest son in a large family of eight boys. David's job was to look after his father's sheep.

David was handsome and brave. His sheep grazed out in the wilderness where wild animals prowled. Once a lion came and stole a lamb from the flock. David chased the lion, caught it by its mane and rescued the lamb from its mouth. Then he killed the lion to protect his sheep.

Another time a big bear tried to take a lamb, David fearlessly went after the bear and rescued the lamb.

David wrote many psalms of praise to God. One psalm speaks about the LORD God being his shepherd – leading him in safe places and providing all his needs.

THINK: The Lord Jesus is the Good Shepherd who gave his life for his sheep – those people who trust in him.

David was a shepherd in his youth and he understood a lot about sheep. In the beautiful Psalm 23 David speaks about the LORD as his shepherd, bringing him to feed in green pastures and to rest by the quiet waters.

Just as a shepherd guides his flock, so the LORD guides his people in paths of righteousness. Through every danger and difficulty, even death, the LORD will help and comfort his people.

The LORD supplies every need. His goodness and love never leave the one who trusts in Him. He will live forever in God's house at last when God takes him to heaven. The Lord Jesus spoke about himself as the Good Shepherd who gave his life for the sheep.

PRAY: Thank the Lord God for giving you the things you need like food and clothing. Thank him also for sending his Son, Jesus, to save sinners. It is through Jesus' sacrifice that his people receive eternal life.

The book of Psalms is the praise book that Jesus would have used. Many were written by David but others by Moses, Asaph and Solomon.

David wrote Psalm 51 to express his sorrow for his sin. He repented and begged for forgiveness. 'I have sinned against you,' he said to God, 'Wash me and I shall be whiter than snow.'

The psalms can help us in every situation. When we are happy we can make a joyful shout to the LORD as Psalm 100 tells us.

When we are in trouble we can get comfort from Psalm 46 'God is our refuge and strength, a very present help in trouble.'

THINK: Psalm 1 gives a lovely picture of the man who delights in the Word of God, the Bible. He is like a tree planted beside a river. It gets plenty water and so produces good fruit. Whatever the righteous man does prospers.

One day Samuel the prophet visited David's home. Samuel was looking for God's choice to be the next king of Israel. One by one David's handsome big brothers were brought to meet Samuel. But God had not chosen any of them.

'Have you no other sons?' Samuel asked Jesse, David's father.

'Yes,' he replied. 'David, the youngest is out looking after the sheep.'

'Fetch him immediately,' ordered Samuel.

David came in from the fields, glowing with good health. God told Samuel, 'This is the one. Anoint him as king.'

Samuel took a container of oil and poured some on David's head, to show that he had been chosen by God to be the future king. All his older brothers watched.

From that day the Spirit of God was with David in a powerful way.

THINK: The Holy Spirit gives spiritual life to believers today. He lives within those who trust in God through Christ.

David's three older brothers were soldiers in Saul's army, fighting the Philistines who wanted to take over the land.

The Philistine army had one soldier who was bigger and stronger than all the others – Goliath was a huge giant over three metres tall. Every morning and evening for forty days Goliath would shout a challenge to the Israelite army on the other side of the valley. 'Choose a man to come and fight me. If I beat your man then you will be our servants.'

Saul and his soldiers, including David's three older brothers, were all scared.

David's father sent him with gifts and to check how his older brothers were getting on in the army camp. As David was talking to his brothers, Goliath appeared across the valley to shout abuse. David was appalled that anyone should defy the army of the living God.

THINK: David knew that God was stronger than any giant. God has all power in heaven and on earth.

David was summoned to meet King Saul. 'I will go and fight this giant Goliath,' he told him bravely. 'You cannot fight against such an experienced soldier,' objected Saul. 'You are just a boy.'

David explained how he had killed a lion and a bear when he was looking after the sheep.

'The same God who helped me then, will help me now.'

Saul agreed to let him fight.

'The LORD be with you,' he said.

David was dressed as a simple shepherd.

'You will need armour,' Saul suggested. 'Use mine.'

He dressed David in his heavy coat of armour and gave him his bronze helmet.

David fastened a sword at his side and then tried to walk around. He could hardly move. They were so heavy and clumsy that David felt very awkward.

'I cannot use these,' he said. 'I am not used to them.' So he took them off.

THINK: David did not use Saul's worldly wisdom to tackle Goliath. He relied completely on God. If we think we can tackle our problems of sin by our own wisdom, we will get into deeper trouble. Only the Lord Jesus can deal with that.

David took his shepherd's staff and his sling and put five smooth pebbles from the stream in his bag. When Goliath saw David coming, he was so angry. He shouted taunts at David.

David bravely replied, 'You come to fight with a sword and a spear and a javelin. But I come to fight in the name of the LORD God. He will help me to win.'

David darted forward to the battle line. He took a stone from his bag, put it in his sling. He slung the stone and it struck Goliath in the middle of his forehead. Goliath fell on his face – dead. With one little stone God's enemy was struck down. David ran to Goliath's body, pulled out the giant's sword from his scabbard and cut off his head.

The Philistine army fled in alarm when they saw their champion was dead. Saul's soldiers chased them for miles. David was a hero.

THINK: Perhaps what David did might seem foolish. But it was God's way. Some people think that the gospel (that Christ died for the ungodly) is foolish, but it is God's way to save sinners.

David and Jonathan, the son of King Saul, became best friends. Jonathan bore no ill will against David, even although he had been chosen to be king after Saul instead of him. Jonathan was David's faithful friend. They made a covenant (or special promise) to be friends always.

Jonathan gave David his robe, his sword, his bow and his belt.

David became a successful soldier and he got promotion in the army ranks. All the people and the soldiers in the army were pleased with David.

Women came out of the towns to meet King Saul, and David and the army coming home. They danced and sang, 'Saul has slain his thousands, and David his tens of thousands.'

Saul was angry about this song which praised David more than him. Saul became jealous of David.

THINK: It is good to have friends, but the best friend of all is the Lord Jesus Christ. He never lets us down.

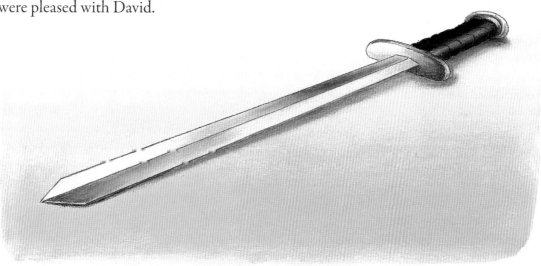

Saul became very jealous of David because he was so popular. Saul hoped David would be killed in battle but God kept him safe.

God was in charge of David's life. In Psalm 27 he said, 'The LORD is my light and salvation. Why should I be afraid of anything?'

David married Michal, Saul's daughter. Michal loved David very much but her father, Saul, hated David.

Saul tried to kill David, even flinging a spear at him as he played music in Saul's house. David managed to dodge the spear.

Saul sent men to David's house to kill him. Michal warned him. She helped him down through the window and he escaped.

Michal put a statue in David's bed with goat's hair on the head. Anyone looking in would think David was asleep.

When Saul found out at last that David was far away, he was very angry with Michal.

THINK: David wrote about God being his light and salvation. Jesus Christ is the light and salvation for all who trust in him. When we are afraid we should trust in the Lord and Saviour, Jesus Christ.

Through all the difficulties, Jonathan was always David's friend, as he had promised.

David was hiding out in the fields, afraid to go near Saul's house. Jonathan agreed to find out if it was safe for David to come. They agreed on a signal.

Jonathan went out to the field with a servant boy. 'Run and find the arrow I shoot,' he told the boy.

Jonathan shot an arrow. As the boy ran to fetch it, Jonathan shouted, 'Is the arrow not beyond you?' That was the signal to David that he had to run away.

'Hurry! Do not delay!' shouted Jonathan.

The boy was sent back to town. David appeared from his hiding place. David and Jonathan renewed their vows of friendship between themselves and their children. Then they parted company.

THINK: David and Jonathan were faithful friends, but they both were faithful to God and put him first. God's command to us, is to love him with all our heart and to love other people as ourselves.

David was on the run from Saul. He escaped to the cave of Adullam. Some of his family and other distressed people joined him. About 400 men were with him.

All the time that Saul was after him God kept David safe. Saul did not harm him.

One day Saul's men camped near David's hideout cave. Saul came into the cave alone not realising that David and his men were further back. 'Kill him,' David's men urged. David refused to do so. But he crept up silently behind Saul and secretly cut off a piece of his robe.

After Saul left the cave, David shouted after him, 'My Lord the king!' Saul turned back. 'I could have killed you today. Look I have the corner of your robe here. Why do you want to harm me? I do not want to harm you.'

Saul was very moved by David's words. 'You are more righteous than I am. You have been good to me, even though I have been bad to you.'

THINK: Jesus has told us to love our enemies and to do good to those who are bad to us (Matthew 5). God gave David the grace to do this.

David and his men protected the shepherds of a rich farmer called Nabal. At sheep-shearing time Nabal made a feast for his workers. David heard about this and sent a message to Nabal, reminding him of their good behaviour and asking if there would be any food for himself and his soldiers.

Nabal was surly and mean. He refused David's request gruffly. David was angry. 'Gird on your swords,' he told his men. They were ready for a fight.

Abigail, Nabal's wife, heard what had happened. She was clever and beautiful. She knew she had to do something to stop trouble. She brought lovely food and wine as a gift for David and his men. She persuaded David not to attack her husband. 'Nabal is a fool,' she said. 'Please forgive us.' David was impressed by Abigail's good sense and gracious words.

Soon after this Nabal died. David asked Abigail to marry him.

THINK: Abigail's wise and gracious words stopped David from the sin of taking revenge. We have the wise gracious Word of God in the Bible. His wise words point us away from sin to the Saviour, the Lord Jesus.

David's spies warned him that Saul and 3,000 men were camped nearby in Ziph.

'Will anyone come down with me to the camp?' David asked. 'I will,' said Abishai.

At dead of night David and Abishai crept past the guards where Saul was sleeping. 'Let me kill him now with just one stroke of my spear,' Abishai urged.

'No, I will not harm the man God has anointed as king,' David replied.

David took the spear and water jug that were beside Saul and got away undetected to the other side of the valley. He shouted from the top of the hill, waking up the guards.

'You have not guarded your king very well! Look, I have his spear and water jug!'

Saul recognised David's voice. He realised David had spared his life again. Saul seemed ashamed of his treatment of David. 'I have sinned,' he confessed. 'I will harm you no more.'

But David knew he was not really safe.

THINK: David waited patiently for God's timing. When he prayed for help in Psalm 31 he admitted, 'My times are in your hands'. It is good for us to pray in that way too.

Saul and his army fought against the Philistines at Mount Gilboa. The fighting was fierce. Jonathan and two of his brothers were killed. Saul fought on but an arrow wounded him critically. He called to his armour-bearer. 'Take a sword and run it through me, or else the Philistines will come and kill me and abuse me.'

The armour-bearer refused to lift the sword. He was terrified. So Saul took his own sword and fell on it. His armour-bearer then did the same.

When news reached David that Saul and Jonathan were dead, he wept and fasted all day. He wrote a special song of lament which was to be taught to the people.

'How the mighty have fallen!
Saul and Jonathan – in life they were
loved and gracious,
And in death they were not parted.
I grieve after you, Jonathan, my brother.
How the mighty have fallen.'

THINK: The Lord Jesus can sympathise with us when we are grieving. He understands how we feel. He himself carries our deepest grief about sin.

129

David asked God what he should do next. 'Go to Hebron,' God told him. David obeyed.

David was anointed king over part of the country called Judah. But one of Saul's sons, Ishbosheth was made king over the rest of the country Israel, in defiance of King David.

For seven-and-a-half years there was war between David and Ishbosheth. Eventually Ishbosheth, was killed. The men of Israel asked David to be their king too.

David ruled over the whole kingdom of Israel and Judah for thirty-three years. The first thing he did as king was to capture the city of Jerusalem. He took the people by surprise by sending his men up a water tunnel into the city.

David made his home in the fortress there. He extended it and it became a great city known as Zion, the city of David. He became more and more powerful because God was with him.

THINK: David was wise to ask for God's guidance. We should pray like David. 'Show me your ways, O LORD. Lead me in your truth'.

David arranged for his men to bring the ark of the covenant to Jerusalem. He wanted God to be the central focus of his kingdom. They put the ark on a new cart. Uzzah and Ahio had the job of guiding the cart. David and his people came behind celebrating with songs and music.

The oxen pulling the cart stumbled. Uzzah reached out and grabbed hold of the ark to stop it falling off. But God was angry with this careless act and Uzzah was struck down dead. David was so afraid he decided to stop the journey and take the ark into a nearby house belonging to Obededom. It remained there for three months. God blessed Obededom and his family because of their care for his ark.

When David heard of God's blessing to Obededom, he thought he would move the ark to Jerusalem. This time he obeyed God's rule and the ark was carried by the men appointed by God for these duties. David was full of joy when the ark was settled in a special tent in Jerusalem. He worshipped God.

THINK: God wants his people to worship him with love from the heart – loving him because he first loved us.

David had a beautiful palace where he lived in peace. One day he said to Nathan the prophet, 'I am living in a palace of cedar wood, while the ark of God remains in a tent.'

Nathan knew what David was thinking; the ark should be housed in a suitable temple. 'Just do it,' Nathan advised, 'The LORD is with you.'

That night God spoke to Nathan with a message for David.

'You will not build a house for me, but one day your son will build a house for my Name. Your house and kingdom will last forever.'

David prayed to the LORD, 'O Sovereign LORD, how great you are. There is no one like you and there is no God but you. Please bless me and my family.'

David was content with making preparations for a temple for God – gathering timber and stone. David eventually passed on instructions about God's house to his son, Solomon.

THINK: God said that he does not live in temples made by man. The whole of the heavens and earth belong to him. We can worship him anywhere.

David made enquiries. 'Is there anyone left from Saul's family, so that I can show him kindness for my friend Jonathan's sake?'

'Jonathan's son, Mephibosheth, is still living,' David was told.

Mephibosheth had been five years old when the word came that his father and grandfather had died in battle. His nurse grabbed him up and hurried to escape but she let him fall. As a result he was lame and could not walk.

David invited Mephibosheth to eat at his royal table.

'Don't be afraid,' David assured him. 'I want to show you kindness.'

David was remembering the promises that he and Jonathan had made to each other years before.

David gave back to Mephibosheth all the land that had belonged to his grandfather Saul. He arranged for servants to work the land for him and bring in the crops. Mephibosheth was always welcome at the king's table.

THINK: God is so kind to us, giving us many gifts that we do not deserve. The best gift of all is Jesus, who satisfies our greatest need, our need of salvation.

David's men were fighting in the war while David remained at home. Late one afternoon he got up from his couch and strolled along the roof of his house. As he looked across the courtyard he saw a beautiful woman having a bath.

'Who is she?' David asked. 'I want her,' he said, even after he found out that she was Bathsheba, the wife of Uriah, one of David's brave soldiers.

Bathsheba was brought to the palace to David. Some time later Bathsheba sent word to David. 'I am expecting a baby.' In a panic David tried to cover up his sin. He arranged for Uriah to get some home leave. But Uriah would not go home to his wife while his comrades were still fighting.

David tried to get Uriah drunk but still he refused. David wrote a letter to Joab the captain. 'Put Uriah in the hottest, fiercest battle.'

Uriah died in the battle just as David had planned. David then married Bathsheba. Had he got away with his sin? No. God was displeased with what David had done.

THINK: Sin always has consequences. It is harmful to ourselves and to others. God hates sin and must punish it.

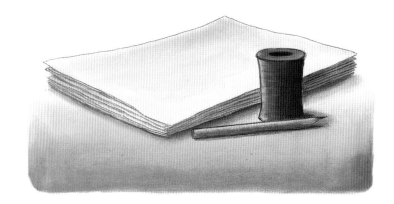

Nathan, God's prophet, was sent to speak to David. He told him a story.

There was a rich man who had lots of flocks and herds. In the same town there was a poor man who had only one little ewe lamb that he loved very much. A traveller came to visit the rich man. Instead of using one of his own flock, the rich man took the poor man's pet lamb and cooked it for dinner.

David was so angry when he heard this story. 'That man deserves to die for doing such a thing.'

'You are the man,' said Nathan. 'God has given you much; yet you have killed Uriah and taken his wife.'

'I have sinned against the LORD,' David confessed. 'Wash me from my iniquity and cleanse me from my sin.'

'The LORD has taken away your sin,' Nathan told him.

THINK: Sin makes us dirty in God's sight. Only he can wash us and make us clean – not with soap and water – but with the precious blood of Jesus, shed for us on Calvary's cross.

David's son, Absalom, was very handsome. He wanted to be the king of Israel and started plotting against his father. When anyone came to the king to settle a dispute, Absalom would meet him first. 'If I were the judge,' he said. 'I would give you justice.'

He became more popular than David. Even some of David's close advisers turned against him. Many fierce battles were fought between David's men and Absalom. At the forest of Ephraim, David's army won a great victory. Absalom was riding through the forest on his mule after the battle. He rode under a tree. His beautiful thick hair got caught in a large branch. The mule trotted on. Absalom was left hanging by his hair. Joab, David's general, came along and killed Absalom even although David had ordered his men not to harm him.

The news was brought to King David – first the good news of the victory then the bad news that Absalom was dead. David was heartbroken.

'My son, my son, Absalom,' he wept. 'If only I had died instead of you.'

THINK: David still loved Absalom even after he had rebelled. God loves rebellious sinners so much that he sent his only Son to die to save them from their sins.

Solomon became king after his father. Solomon's reign was a time of peace and prosperity. One day he went to the holy place at Gibeon to offer sacrifices to God.

God appeared to him in a dream that night and said, 'Ask for whatever you want me to give you.'

Solomon's answer pleased God. 'Give me wisdom and knowledge,' he said, 'so that I can guide the people and judge between right and wrong.'

God gave Solomon the wisdom he asked for and also riches and honour and the promise of a long life if he obeyed God's laws.

Solomon possessed hundreds of chariots and thousands of horses. Silver and gold were as plentiful as stones in Jerusalem. The news about his wealth and wisdom spread all over the land and to the neighbouring countries.

THINK: Solomon wrote many proverbs which teach us how to live. 'The fear of the LORD,' he tells us, 'is the beginning of wisdom.' If we want to be wise, we have to start by giving God the respect and honour that he is due.

One day Solomon's wisdom was put to the test. Two women came to him, both claiming to be the mother of the same baby boy.

One of the women explained to Solomon, 'We live in the same house. I had a baby and this women had a baby three days later. This woman's child died in the night and she came and stole my baby while I slept. She laid her dead child by me.'

The other woman denied this. 'No, I am the living baby's mother.'

Solomon said, 'Bring me a sword. We will divide the child in two and give you half each.'

The first woman cried out, 'Oh, no, give her the child, please do not kill him!' Solomon then knew that she was the real mother. He gave the baby to her.

THINK: God had given Solomon the gift of great wisdom. God has given us many gifts, but the greatest gift of all is Jesus, God's Son. Through him we have eternal life.

During the fourth year of his reign, Solomon began to build the temple. The house of the LORD was about thirty metres long, ten metres broad, and fifteen metres high. It was built of stone already prepared so that there was no sound of cutting or hammering on the site.

The walls, floor and ceilings were made of cedar wood. The whole place was covered with pure gold as well as the altar. The building was magnificent inside and out. The decoration and furnishings were wonderful. It took seven years for the thousands of workers to complete the task.

The ark of the covenant was brought into the temple by the priests. The glory of the LORD filled the temple. The priests could not continue ministering because of this glory.

Solomon blessed all the congregation of Israel and prayed, 'O LORD God, there is no God like you – hear from heaven, and when you hear, forgive.'

THINK: God is the same today. He loves to hear his children pray to him. He longs to give forgiveness to those who repent.

Solomon also built a wonderful palace for himself – made from gold and precious materials. This took thirteen years to complete. This building was magnificent, nothing had been seen like it before.

The Queen of Sheba heard about Solomon's wealth and wisdom. She decided to see for herself if these reports were true. She arrived with a train of camels carrying many gifts for Solomon. She asked Solomon lots of hard questions. Nothing was too hard for him to explain to her. God had given him special wisdom. The Queen of Sheba was very impressed with Solomon's wisdom and wealth. 'I heard about you in my own country: but not even half was told me,' she said to Solomon. 'Praise to the LORD your God who has delighted in you and made you rule over Israel.'

She left for home, amazed at all she had seen and heard.

THINK: Jesus tells us that he is even greater than Solomon. We should be more amazed at Jesus' wisdom, than the Queen of Sheba was when she met Solomon.

When Solomon grew old he turned away from God. He had married many foreign wives and Solomon began to worship their heathen gods. God was very angry with Solomon for this. 'After you are gone,' God told him, 'the kingdom will be torn from your family. But because of your father, David, I will allow your son to be king of one tribe.'

After Solomon died, his son, Rehoboam, became king. The people rebelled against him because he made them work like slaves. The Israelites in the north of the kingdom wanted Jeroboam as their king. But the tribes of Judah and Benjamin remained loyal to Rehoboam, the grandson of David.

The kingdom was divided, just as God had said, into Israel in the north and the smaller kingdom of Judah in the south.

THINK: We need the Lord's care and keeping every day. If we forget to trust in him, it is so easy to fall into sin.

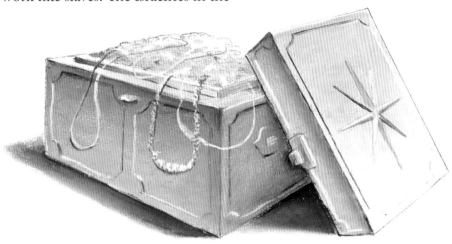

Jeroboam was a bad king. He led the people of Israel into sin. One day his son became sick. Jeroboam told his wife, 'Disguise yourself so that no one will know you are the queen. Go to the prophet Ahijah in Shiloh with some gifts. Ask him if the boy will recover.'

Ahijah was old and blind, but the LORD told him who was coming before she arrived. 'Come in, wife of Jeroboam,' he called out. 'Why are you pretending to be someone else?'

He then told Jeroboam's wife to tell her husband from God. 'Because you have not obeyed my commands, disaster will come to your family. Not only will your boy die, but all your other sons who are well.'

THINK: God has to punish sin. Jesus has suffered for the sins of those who trust in him. He took the punishment for sin when he died on the cross.

After Solomon died, the kingdom was divided into two – Israel and a smaller country, Judah. Many of the kings of both countries forgot about God and did evil things.

One of the worst was King Ahab. He and his wicked wife, Jezebel, worshipped a false god, Baal.

Elijah was a good man who loved the LORD God. God used him to speak to Ahab and the people of Israel.

One day God told Elijah to warn King Ahab, 'There will be no rain or dew on the land for some years.' Ahab was angry at this bad news.

'Go east across the River Jordan and hide beside the brook Cherith,' God told Elijah.

Elijah drank water from the brook. Every morning and every evening ravens brought bread and meat for him to eat. God took care of Elijah in this lonely place.

THINK: God takes care of us too. Every bite of food we eat is a gift from God. Let's remember to thank him.

God told Elijah to go to a place called Zarephath.

'A widow who lives there will give you some food,' God told him. Elijah met the woman gathering up sticks, at the city gate.

'Bring me a drink of water and a piece of bread,' Elijah asked her.

'I have hardly any food left,' she said. 'I am about to cook one last meal for myself and my son before we die of starvation.'

'Make a little cake for me first,' Elijah persuaded her. 'God has told me that your barrel of flour and your jug of oil will last as long as this drought lasts.'

The woman did as Elijah asked. There was enough food for Elijah and the woman and her family every day. The barrel of flour and the jug of oil lasted for as long as it was needed.

THINK: The woman's kindness was rewarded. We are told in the Bible to be kind to one another, remembering how kind the Lord Jesus is to us in forgiving our sin.

One day the widow who had helped Elijah came to him in great distress. Her son had become ill. He grew worse and worse and eventually died. Elijah carried the boy upstairs to a bed in the room he had used. He stretched himself out on top of the boy's body three times and prayed that the LORD would bring him back to life.

God heard Elijah's prayers. The boy's life returned to him. Elijah picked him up and carried him downstairs to his mother.

'Look,' he said, 'your son is alive.'

The woman was overjoyed. 'Now I know that you are a man of God. The words of God that you speak are really true.'

The woman had done what she could by helping Elijah when he was hungry. God had used Elijah to help her in her time of trouble.

THINK: The widow knew to go to the man of God to help her in trouble. When we are in trouble, we should remember to ask God for help. He will give grace to help in time of need.

145

King Ahab and Queen Jezebel still worshipped the false god, Baal. They hated God and his prophets. Ahab called Elijah a troublemaker. 'You are the troublemaker,' Elijah told him, 'by worshipping Baal instead of God.'

'Let's have a contest,' challenged Elijah, 'between me and the prophets of Baal.'

Ahab summoned all the Israelites and 450 prophets of Baal to Mount Carmel. The God who accepted a sacrifice of a bull by sending fire would prove to be the true, powerful God.

The prophets of Baal had their turn first. They took a bull and prepared it as a sacrifice on the altar. Then they danced round praying to Baal. Nothing happened.

At noon Elijah made fun of them. 'Perhaps Baal is busy or sleeping. Shout louder!'

The prophets of Baal shouted louder and louder till the middle of the afternoon. Still nothing happened. Baal had failed. Now it was Elijah's turn – but the altar of the Lord had not been kept in good repair. So first he had to repair the altar before he could go any further.

THINK: It is no surprise that Baal failed. The Lord God who gave us his Word, the Bible, is the only true, powerful God.

When the altar of the Lord had been repaired with twelve big stones, Elijah dug a trench around it. He put wood on the altar and then laid the prepared bull on it. 'Fill four jars with water and pour them over the offering and the wood,' he ordered.

The order was repeated twice more until the wood and offering were soaking wet and the trench was filled with water.

Elijah prayed to God 'O Lord, prove that you are the true God and that I am your servant. Answer me, so that the people will know that you are God.'

The Lord sent down fire on the altar. It burnt up the sacrifice, wood, stones and soil, and dried up the water in the trench. When the people saw this they threw themselves on the ground and shouted, 'The Lord is God! The Lord is God!' The Lord had proved without doubt that he was the true God.

THINK: The one true God is the same God as he was for Elijah. He can hear and answer your prayers too.

Jezebel was furious when she heard what had happened to the prophets of Baal. She vowed to kill Elijah. He fled for his life. Eventually he reached Sinai where he hid in a cave.

God asked him, 'What are you doing here?'

Elijah replied, 'I am the only one left who serves the LORD. People are trying to kill me.'

'Go and stand on top of the mountain,' God told Elijah.

A fierce wind blew and shattered the rocks. Then there was an earthquake, then a fire. But the LORD did not use these powerful forces to speak to Elijah. He spoke in a gentle whisper. Elijah covered his face with his cloak.

God told Elijah that he was not the only one who served the LORD. 'There are still 7,000 people alive in Israel who serve me,' said God.

Elijah should not have been so sad.

THINK: There are millions of people all over the world who trust in the Lord Jesus Christ. They are all part of one family, although they come from different nations. Jesus Christ is their elder brother.

Ahab had plenty of possessions but he really wanted a vineyard belonging to Naboth. Naboth did not think it right to sell his family property. So Ahab sulked.

'What's the matter?' asked Jezebel. 'Cheer up! I'll get you the vineyard.'

So she plotted and wrote letters to the city leaders ordering them to accuse Naboth of cursing God and the king. They obeyed her orders, so Naboth was falsely accused and put to death. Ahab took the vineyard for himself.

God sent Elijah to warn Ahab about the results of this evil behaviour. 'God will punish you,' warned Elijah. Sin always leads to trouble.

THINK: In the tenth commandment God tells us not to covet what belongs to other people. We should learn to be content in every situation, trusting in the Lord Jesus as our strength.

King Ahab wanted to invade a neighbouring country to win back a city. He asked Jehoshaphat, King of Judah, to help him. 'I'll gladly help you,' he said, 'but we should ask the LORD first to see what we should do.'

Ahab summoned his heathen prophets. They all agreed that Ahab would win a great victory.

'Is there not a prophet of the LORD that we can consult?' Jehoshaphat asked.

Micaiah was sent for. 'Tell the king the same as the others,' he was told.

'I will only say what the LORD tells me,' said Micaiah. 'The others are telling lies. Going to war will bring disaster.'

Ahab was so annoyed. 'He never prophesies any good to me. It's always bad.'

One of the other prophets walked over to Micaiah and slapped him in the face. Micaiah was put in jail.

THINK: Brave Micaiah told the unpopular truth because he was trusting in God. Jesus who is 'the truth' will help his people to speak what is true and helpful.

Ahab and Jehoshaphat did not listen to Micaiah. They led their armies off to battle against Syria. Jehoshaphat wore his royal robes but Ahab decided to go dressed as an ordinary soldier.

The King of Syria commanded his captains to fight no one except King Ahab. When they saw Jehoshaphat in his royal robes they immediately thought, 'That's the man we're after,' but when Jehoshaphat shouted out who he was they turned back.

Someone shot an arrow at random which struck Ahab in a gap in his armour. He was badly wounded and later in the evening he died.

THINK: No man, not even a king, can win against God's plans. He reigns over all.

God told Elijah to choose Elisha to succeed him. Elisha agreed. Elijah knew he would soon go to heaven. 'What can I do for you before I am taken away?' he asked Elisha.

'Let me have a double share of your spirit,' Elisha replied. Elisha wanted double the amount of mighty power that Elijah had.

'You will receive it only if you see me as I am taken up to heaven.'

They kept talking as they walked along. Suddenly a chariot of fire, pulled by horses of fire, came between them. Elijah was taken up to heaven by a whirlwind.

Elisha saw this wonderful happening. He picked up Elijah's cloak and carried it to the bank of the Jordan river. He struck the river twice with the cloak. The water divided and Elisha walked over to the other side. God's power was now with him.

THINK: God's power is the same today. The gospel is described as the power of God which brings all who believe it to heaven.

One day a poor widow came to Elisha for help. 'My husband is dead. He owed some money to a man. My sons are going to be sold as slaves to pay the debt.'

'How can I help you?' replied Elisha. 'What do you have in the house?'

'All I have is a little oil,' she said.

'Go and ask your neighbours to lend you lots of empty jars. Go into your house with your sons and shut the door. Pour the oil into the jars. As each is filled, put it to one side.'

The woman kept pouring the oil into the jars. Only when all the jars were filled, did the oil stop. Then she sold the jars of oil and was able to pay all her debts. There was enough money left over for the widow and her sons to live comfortably.

THINK: God, the creater of the oil, worked a miracle to help the poor woman. Everything is under God's control.

153

Elisha travelled a lot. In the town of Shunem he would stay with a rich couple who had prepared a little room for him. When Elisha found out that the couple had no children he told the woman that she would have a baby in about a year's time.

A year later she gave birth to a son. The boy grew strong and fit until one morning he was in the fields with his father. Suddenly he called out, 'My head, my head!'

'Carry him home to his mother,' his father told a servant. The sick boy sat on his mother's knee till noon and then he died. The heart-broken mother carried him to Elisha's bed. Then she fetched Elisha to her house.

Elisha went into the room and shut the door. He prayed to the LORD. He stretched himself on top of the boy. Soon the boy's body grew warm. Elisha once more stretched out on the boy. This time the boy sneezed seven times and opened his eyes. God had answered Elisha's prayer. How thankful the mother was to have her boy restored to life.

THINK: Jesus conquered death when he rose from the dead. All who believe in him have eternal life with him in heaven.

Naaman, a commander in the Syrian army, had leprosy, a terrible skin disease. A servant girl who had been captured from Samaria suggested that he go to the prophet Elisha, to be cured.

When he arrived, Elisha sent out a messenger to tell him to wash in the River Jordan seven times. Naaman was not impressed. 'I have better rivers at home,' he argued.

However, his servants persuaded him to listen to the advice and when Naaman came out of the river for the seventh time his skin was as smooth as a baby's. What a miracle! Naaman was delighted.

He went back to Elisha and confessed, 'The God of Israel is the only true God.'

THINK: Cleansing from sin comes through faith in Christ. This may seem foolish to some people, but it is God's way and it works.

147. The Floating Axe - 2 Kings 6

One day the group of prophets who followed Elisha told him. 'The place where we meet is too small. Let us go down beside the River Jordan, where there are plenty of logs, to build a new place.'

Elisha gave his permission and agreed to go with them. At the Jordan men began cutting down the trees. As one of them was chopping, the axe head fell into the river. The man was so upset. 'It was not my axe. It was borrowed from someone else.'

'Where did it fall?' Elisha asked.

The young man showed him the exact spot. Elisha cut a stick and threw it into the water. The axe head rose to the surface and floated. 'Grab it,' said Elisha.

The young man was able to retrieve the borrowed axe head.

THINK: What an amazing miracle showing God's power over all his creation and his care for his people.

King Ahaziah of Judah was a bad king. He did not love and serve God. He was killed by his enemies when his son, Joash, was just a baby. Athaliah, Joash's grandmother, was evil too. She decided to kill all her family, including Joash, so that she could be made queen.

Joash's aunt, Jehosheba, took him away secretly and hid him with his nurse in a bedroom in the temple. Jehosheba and her husband, Jehoiada, the priest, looked after Joash carefully for six years. He was the rightful king, but for six years Athaliah ruled the land.

Jehoiada made a plan to put Joash on the throne. He sent for the commanders of the army and asked them to stand guard with all the men at the temple. Jehoiada brought the seven-year old Joash out of the temple, put the crown on his head and announced that he was the king. He was anointed with oil, the people clapped their hands and shouted, 'Long live the king!'

THINK: God used Joash's aunt to keep him safe till he could become a king. This was God's plan. God has a plan for your life too.

When wicked Athaliah heard the noise of people cheering and shouting, 'Long live the king!' she hurried over to the temple. There she saw Joash standing by a pillar with the king's crown on his head.

'Treason! Treason!' she screamed, tearing her clothes in fury. Jehoiada ordered the soldiers to seize her. She was taken from the temple area and put to death. Joash and the people had nothing to fear because Athaliah was gone.

Joash reigned in Judah for forty years. With Jehoiada's help and guidance he was a good king. Jehoiada drew up a covenant between the LORD God and the king and the people that they would be God's people.

Joash made arrangements for the temple to be repaired. It had been damaged during his grandmother's reign.

Sadly, after Jehoiada died, Joash listened to bad advisers and turned away from the true God.

THINK: We need to continually trust in God and listen to the good advice in his Word. The armour of God protects us from the devil who wants us to turn away from God.

Uzziah was sixteen years old when he became King of Judah. He did what was right and God made him prosper.

Zechariah the priest instructed him to fear the LORD and obey his Word. He built towers and fortresses in Jerusalem and in the desert. He dug wells to find water for his animals. He had farms and vineyards which he loved.

Uzziah had a powerful army and skilful men made machines for the army to shoot arrows and hurl stones from the towers.

He became famous but grew very proud. This led him to go into the temple and perform the duties which only the priests were allowed to do.

When the priests bravely challenged him he was furious. Even the king has to obey God.

As a punishment the LORD gave Uzziah the skin disease leprosy.

He had to live in isolation till the day of his death.

THINK: The sin of pride often troubles us too. Only the love of God, through Jesus Christ, can help us not to be boastful or proud. The Bible tells us that we should boast in one thing only and that is the Lord Jesus Christ.

Hezekiah became king in Judah. He did what was right like his ancestor, David, not like his father, Ahaz. Hezekiah realised that God was displeased with Ahaz's behaviour. The temple had been neglected and the worship of God abandoned. Hezekiah wanted to change all that.

He sent priests into the temple to clean it. They started with the inner room, then the outer court. The job was done in sixteen days.

The next day Hezekiah went to the temple with the city officials to present sacrifices to the LORD. The priests carried out the consecration ceremonies to make atonement for the sins of the nation.

Everyone worshipped the LORD, singing psalms. Trumpets blew. People from all over the country brought sacrifices and thank offerings.

Hezekiah and the people were so happy about what God had done, in restoring the temple so quickly.

THINK: God wants us to worship him with all our heart, soul, strength and mind.

Hezekiah sent word all round the country inviting people to come to the temple in Jerusalem to celebrate the Passover Feast (the feast remembering how God had saved his people from slavery in Egypt). This feast had been forgotten for many years.

'Come back to the LORD God,' the king's letter said. 'God is full of kindness and mercy.'

Some people laughed at the letter and refused to come. But many wanted to obey God's command and huge crowds gathered in Jerusalem and celebrated the Passover with great joy.

The priests and Levites praised the LORD with cymbals and singing (which King Hezekiah greatly appreciated.)

All the heathen altars in Jerusalem had been knocked down before the Passover Feast and afterwards the people travelled all over Judah and tore down all the idol altars and images.

THINK: God's kindness and mercy to us today give us great joy, causing us to praise and thank him.

153. Hezekiah trusts in God - 2 Kings 19, 2 Chronicles 32

Hezekiah was faithful to God and did what was right. So God blessed him.

The King of Assyria invaded Judah. Hezekiah did all he could to defend Jerusalem but the people were frightened. 'Be brave,' Hezekiah urged. 'The Assyrians have a big army but we have God on our side to help us and fight our battles.'

The King of Assyria tried to frighten Hezekiah. 'No other army has defeated us. Why should you be any different?' he shouted. He also sent a letter to Hezekiah insulting God. When Hezekiah read the letter, he took it up to the temple and spread it out before the LORD. He prayed to God for help.

That night the angel of the LORD went through the Assyrian camp and destroyed the Assyrian army. The king had to go back home in disgrace. Hezekiah's God had delivered him from the enemy. Many people brought gifts to Jerusalem to express their thanks to God.

THINK: When we have a problem it is best to take it to God in prayer and ask him for help.

162

Hezekiah became very sick. Isaiah the prophet went to visit him. 'Get your affairs in order and prepare to die,' Isaiah said to him.

Hezekiah turned his face to the wall and pleaded with God, weeping. Before Isaiah had left the courtyard, God told him to go back to Hezekiah. 'Tell him God has heard his prayer and will heal him. In three days he will be out of bed and at the temple. I will add fifteen years to his life.'

Isaiah told Hezekiah to apply a paste of cooked figs to his boil. Hezekiah recovered. 'Do a miracle to prove to me that the LORD has really healed me,' Hezekiah asked Isaiah.

So Isaiah agreed. 'Do you want the shadow on the sundial to go forward ten degrees or back?'

'The shadow always goes forward,' Hezekiah said, 'make it go back.' So Isaiah asked the LORD to do this, and God graciously answered his prayers.

THINK: God's grace to Hezekiah was immense. His grace to us is immense too. He gave us his Son to die in our place so that we would live eternally.

Manasseh became king after his father, Hezekiah, had died. He was only twelve years old. He was a very bad king. He encouraged the people to worship idols. He rebuilt the heathen altars that his father had destroyed. He even went so far as to build heathen altars in the temple of the LORD, and do all sorts of wicked deeds.

The LORD was very angry with this evil, but Manasseh and the people ignored God's warnings.

God sent the Assyrian army. Manasseh was seized, bound up with chains and carted off to Babylon.

At last he came to his senses and cried out to God for help. The LORD listened and answered his prayers. Manasseh returned to his kingdom. He finally realised that the LORD was the one true God.

God can save the worst of sinners.

THINK: No one is too young to be saved and no one is too old. No one is too bad and no one is too good. We all need God and his salvation through Jesus Christ.

When Manasseh returned to Jerusalem he made big changes in the kingdom. He removed the false gods, he took the idols out of the temple. He rebuilt the altar of the LORD and offered peace offerings and thanksgiving offerings, and commanded the people to worship the LORD God.

When Manasseh died, his son, Amon, reigned, but only for two years. It was an evil reign like his father's was at first. But he did not change like Manasseh. He grew worse and worse. At last his own officers could stand it no more and assassinated him.

His son, Josiah, then became king when he was eight years old.

THINK: Manasseh repented when he turned from his sin with sorrow and instead wanted to love and serve God. Repentance is a gift from God.

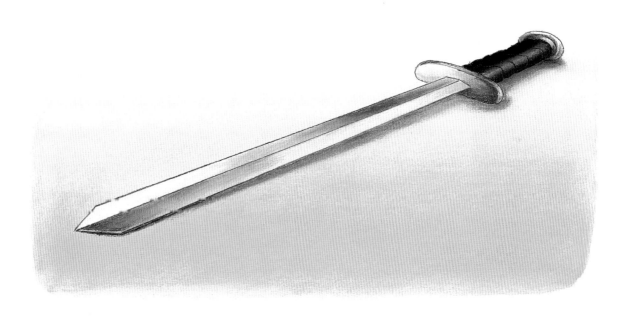

Josiah was only eight years old when he became king. He was a good king, carefully following the example of King David.

When he was sixteen he began to seek God. He pulled down the heathen altars and idols all around the country. He came to realise how sinful idol worship was. Then he turned his attention to the temple. It needed to be repaired. Money was collected to pay for the work of the carpenters and stonemasons, and to buy stone and timber for the temple that had been allowed to fall into ruin.

One day Hilkiah the priest found an old scroll which turned out to be the laws of God as given to Moses. When King Josiah heard the Law of God read out, he was so upset. 'God will surely punish us,' he said, 'we have not obeyed these laws of God.'

THINK: God has given us his Word, the Bible. It is wrong to neglect or ignore God's Word. Everything we are required to believe is found in the Bible.

King Josiah summoned all the people great and small, the elders, the priests and the Levites to the temple.

There the king read the scroll to them – the law of God that Hilkiah had found in the temple.

King Josiah made a vow to the LORD, before all the people, to follow God's commandments with all his heart and soul and to obey what was written in the scroll.

He then asked all the citizens of Jerusalem and the land of Benjamin to promise to follow God too. From then until the end of Josiah's reign, they continued to serve Jehovah their God, and to obey his commands.

THINK: The Bible tells us all about God – the Father, the Son and the Holy Spirit, and how we should serve him.

3. Prophets, a Prophetess, a Queen and a Priest

Books of the Bible:

1 Chronicles, Ezra, Nehemiah, Esther, Job, Psalms, Proverbs,
Isaiah, Jeremiah, Ezekiel, Daniel, Jonah, Luke

What you will read about:

Huldah, Jeremiah, Isaiah, Daniel,
The Exile, The Return from Exile,
Esther, Job, Solomon,
Ezekiel, Jonah, Zechariah.

Hilkiah the priest and some other men went to consult Huldah the prophetess. They told her how sad the king was and how worried he was about not obeying God's law. Huldah gave them a message from God. 'God is angry with sin and will punish disobedience.'

The special message to Josiah gave him a little comfort. 'Because you are sorry for the sin and have humbled yourself before God, then the punishment will not come in your lifetime.'

Hilkiah and the others listened carefully and went back to King Josiah with this word from the LORD.

THINK: God hates sin and has to punish it because he is just. God placed the punishment for sin on his Son, Jesus Christ. Jesus took the punishment for sinners.

While Josiah was king, Jeremiah was a priest in Anathoth in the land of Benjamin. God spoke an important message to Jeremiah.

'I have known you before you were born. I want you to be a special messenger for me to the world.'

'O Lord God,' exclaimed Jeremiah. 'I cannot do that. I am far too young.'

'Don't say that,' said God. 'You will go where I send you and speak whatever I tell you to. Don't be afraid. I will be with you.'

God touched Jeremiah's mouth and said, 'I will put my words in your mouth.'

God told Jeremiah that the kingdom of Judah would be destroyed. He had to warn the people. God told Jeremiah that the king and officials would work against him. 'They will fail,' God assured him, 'for I am with you. I will deliver you.'

THINK: The Lord is with his people today too. He has promised never to leave them. They should therefore not be afraid.

God told Jeremiah to write down all the words that he had spoken to him. 'Perhaps when the people hear about the punishment I plan for them,' God said, 'they will turn from their sins and I will forgive them.'

So Jeremiah dictated all the words and his friend, Baruch, wrote them down on the scroll. Jeremiah sent Baruch to read God's words to all the people in the Temple. Word was sent to the important officials in the palace. King Jehoiakim wanted to hear for himself. He ordered Jehudi to get the scroll and read it to him while he sat beside the fire.

After Jehudi had read three or four leaves, the king took them, not to pore over God's words more closely, but he took a penknife, angrily cut the pages into pieces and threw them on to the fire.

But God's words could not be destroyed like that. Jeremiah dictated the words all over again to Baruch. We still have these words in the book of Jeremiah in the Bible.

THINK: The whole Bible is the Word of God. We should read it carefully and often. It tells us the good news of what the Lord Jesus Christ has done and how we should live.

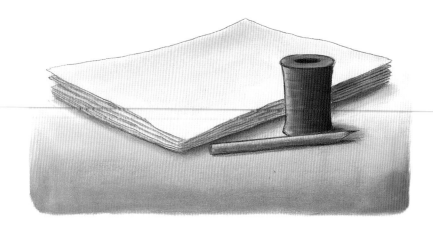

King Zedekiah and the people of Jerusalem did not want to listen to Jeremiah's warning from God. 'Jeremiah is upsetting the soldiers and the people,' the officials told the king.

So with the king's permission, they lowered Jeremiah with ropes down a deep well in the courtyard. The well had no water – only mud. Jeremiah was out of the way. They did not hear his warnings now. When Ebedmelech, one of the officials, heard what had happened he went to see the king.

'Set Jeremiah free, before he starves to death,' said Ebedmelech. The king agreed. Kind Ebedmelech took thirty men to help him. He dropped down some old rags and worn-out clothes to protect his armpits from chafing by the ropes. Ebedmelech and his helpers pulled Jeremiah out of the muddy pit. Jeremiah was confined to the courtyard but still faithfully proclaimed God's Words.

THINK: The Lord God is present everywhere. He is caring for his people even in the deepest trouble.

Isaiah saw a vision of the LORD seated on a throne. Above him were seraphs with six wings – two covering their faces, two covering their feet and with two they were flying. They were calling out, 'Holy, holy, holy is the LORD Almighty; the whole earth is full of His glory.' The temple was filled with smoke. Isaiah was greatly affected by this vision. 'Woe is me!' he cried. 'I am a man with sinful lips and live with people who have sinful lips.'

One of the seraphs took a burning coal from the altar and touched Isaiah's mouth. 'Your guilt has been taken away.'

God then said, 'Whom shall I send? Who will go?'

Isaiah answered, 'Here am I. Send me.'

So God sent Isaiah to be his messenger to his people.

THINK: Messengers still take God's Word to other people. Preachers, missionaries and many Christians, young and old, tell the gospel of the Lord Jesus wherever they can.

Isaiah's message pointed to the coming Messiah – the special king that the Jews expected God to send. Isaiah told of his birth 'To us a child is born, to us a son is given . . . he will be called Wonderful, Counsellor, Mighty God, Everlasting Father, Prince of Peace.' Isaiah's words came true when the Lord Jesus was born. He is God the Son who reigns over all the world, a prince and a saviour.

Isaiah also prophesied about Jesus' death. His suffering and pain and rejection are all detailed. He explains that his death was a sacrifice to bring forgiveness to his people. 'He was pierced for our transgressions,' says Isaiah, 'He was bruised for our iniquities.' Isaiah even foretold that Jesus would die along with wicked men and that his grave would belong to a rich man. Jesus died on the cross between two thieves and laid in the tomb belonging to rich Joseph of Arimathea.

PRAY: Thank God the Father for planning salvation from before time began. Thank him for how he has given us his Word the Bible. Thank him for the message of salvation that we find in his Word.

165. Jerusalem Attacked - Jeremiah 39

Jeremiah faithfully spoke God's message, even though people did not like what they heard. King Zedekiah was warned that the king of Babylon would capture the city and destroy it. He still did not want to listen to God's message.

King Nebuchadnezzar and his army came against Jerusalem and besieged it for two years. Eventually the resistance was weakened and they got through the city wall and the city fell into their hands. The palace and houses were burned down. The treasures from the temple were stolen and then the temple was burned.

King Zedekiah fled during the night, but he was caught and brought before King Nebuchadnezzar. Zedekiah watched as his children and nobles were killed. Then he was blinded and taken away captive to Babylon.

Many people were taken to be slaves in Babylon but Jeremiah stayed in Judah.

THINK: Jeremiah remained faithful to God even when life was difficult. He knew that God is always faithful to his people.

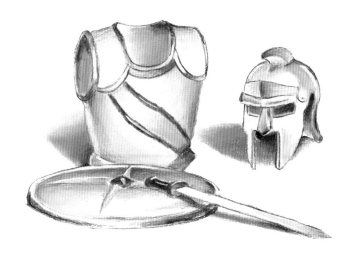

Daniel was a fine young man, born into a noble family in Judah. King Nebuchadnezzar of Babylon and his army defeated the army of Judah. He took away treasures from the temple and captured many fine young men. One of the exiles was Daniel.

The king selected Daniel and three of his friends to be trained to work in the royal palace. They were strong, handsome and clever. They learned the new language and were able to read all the important books.

They were offered the best food and wine from the king's table. But they refused, asking instead for vegetables and water that would not conflict with their worship of God. The guard was unhappy about it but when he saw how healthy Daniel and his friends looked, he let them keep to their simple diet.

God and his law were very important to Daniel.

THINK: God's law, the Bible, is perfect. It tells us what to believe about God and shows us the Lord Jesus.

King Nebuchadnezzar had a strange dream which worried him. None of his wise men could explain it. He was so angry, he wanted to kill them. When Daniel heard of this, he asked, 'Can you give me some time to try to interpret the dream?'

Daniel urged his friends to pray with him for help to solve the mystery. During the night God revealed the answer to Daniel in a vision.

He was so thankful to God, 'I praise and thank you, O God. You have made known to me what we asked.'

Daniel went to the king. 'God has shown me this mystery,' he said. 'This is what will happen.'

Daniel told the dream in detail and explained its meaning. The king was so impressed that he fell down before Daniel. 'Surely your God is the God of gods and the King of kings,' he declared.

Daniel was put in charge of all the wise men.

THINK: We can pray to God for help at any time too. We should pray that the Lord would forgive us for our sins.

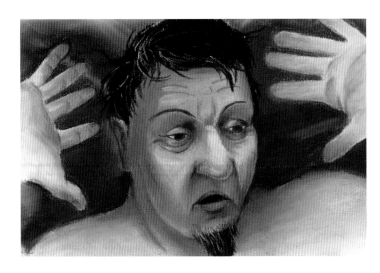

Nebuchadnezzar made a huge statue of gold. 'Everyone must bow down and worship this statue,' he ordered.

Daniel's friends, Shadrach, Meshach and Abednego would not. They loved and worshipped the one true God. The king was furious. 'Throw them into a burning fiery furnace,' the king ordered.

'Our God is able to save us,' the friends said. 'But even if he doesn't, we will not bow down to a statue.'

The furnace was heated seven times hotter than usual, and the men were thrown in.

As the king watched, he jumped up in amazement. 'We threw three men into the fire but I see four men walking, unhurt. The fourth looks like the Son of God.'

The friends walked out unhurt, with not even the smell of burning on their clothes. The king was impressed. 'Blessed be God who saved his servants.'

THINK: God is able to save anyone, anywhere. Jesus is the Saviour. He was given the name Jesus, because he would save his people from their sins.

King Belshazzar made a great feast for a thousand of his noblemen. While they were drinking wine, he ordered the servant to fetch the gold and silver goblets that his father had taken from the temple in Jerusalem. In the middle of the drunken party, a strange thing happened.

The finger of a hand appeared and wrote on the wall. Belshazzar was alarmed. His face turned pale. His knees knocked together. His wise men could not tell what the strange words meant.

Daniel was summoned to the king. 'I can tell you what it means,' he said. 'You have set yourself up against God. God has sent you this message.

'Your reign will soon be at an end. You fall short of God's standards. Your kingdom will be conquered and given to someone else.'

That very night Belshazzar was killed and Darius from Media took over the country.

God's warning had indeed happened.

THINK: It is very sad and dangerous to oppose the Lord God. He is worthy of honour and praise! God has warned us too that we are not to ignore the free gift of God's salvation.

King Darius promoted Daniel to be chief administrator to the whole land. The other officials were jealous. They wanted to get rid of him but Daniel was honest and a good worker.

The officials knew that Daniel prayed three times a day to the LORD so they hatched a plot against Daniel. They went to see King Darius. 'We think you should make a law, O king, saying that any man who prays to any god or man, except you during the next thirty days, should be thrown into the lions' den.'

The king was flattered and agreed to do as they suggested. Daniel heard about the new law, but refused to obey it. He went straight to his room, knelt by his open window and prayed to God as usual.

THINK: Jesus prayed often and sometimes all night. We should pray to God whenever we can.

The jealous officials were delighted to catch Daniel breaking the new law. They immediately told the king. King Darius was upset, but the law could not be changed. Daniel was thrown into the den with the fierce lions. A big stone was placed over the entrance. There was no way out.

The king was miserable. 'May your God, whom you are always serving, rescue you,' he said to Daniel.

The next morning the king hurried to the den. He called out, 'Daniel, has your God been able to save you from the lions?' To his great joy, Daniel shouted back, 'My God sent his angels to shut the lions' mouths. They have not hurt me at all.'

Daniel was lifted out of the lions' den without even a scratch. God had kept him safe in a very dangerous place. Darius put an order throughout the land. 'Everyone must fear and honour the God that Daniel serves. He is the living God.'

THINK: Daniel put God first in his life. Do you trust Jesus and serve him? The Lord is willing to save all who come to him by faith.

God's people were sad to be living in exile away from their own land. But they were given plenty of time to be sorry for their past sins of forgetting God.

They longed to be back in their own land. One psalm that they sang told of their longing to be home.

'We sat and wept beside the rivers of Babylon, when we thought about Jerusalem. We hanged our harps on the willow trees. How difficult to sing about the LORD when we are prisoners in a foreign land. We will never forget Jerusalem.'

God did not forget them. He was preparing a plan for their return.

THINK: Jesus never forgets the person who believes in him. 'I will never leave you, or forsake you,' he promises.

The King of Persia conquered Babylon. This had an important result for the people of God exiled there. God told King Cyrus to let his people go back to Jerusalem. They had been in exile for seventy years.

'God has commanded me to rebuild the temple in Jerusalem,' Cyrus announced to the people. All the Jews can return to help rebuild the temple. Those who do not go should help with expenses, giving clothing and supplies and money for the temple funds.

King Cyrus gave back the gold bowls and other treasures that had been stolen from the temple seventy years before.

How happy God's people must have been to be returning home.

THINK: The people gave generously to the work of rebuilding the temple. God wants us to give to the work of his church, not grudgingly, but gladly. God loves us to give cheerfully.

The first task was to rebuild the altar of God on its old site. The altar was then used to sacrifice offerings to God. Once the building had started and the foundations were complete, most people sang praise to God. 'God is good, his love and mercy to Israel will last forever.'

Only some of the old men who remembered Solomon's beautiful temple, were disappointed with the new one. Some foreigners who had settled in Judah tried to upset the work. They even wrote to the king trying to stir up trouble. But the work went ahead successfully, encouraged by the prophets of God, Haggai and Zechariah.

Ezra the priest was a wise leader as the temple was completed. He had studied God's Law and always tried to obey it. The LORD God blessed him.

THINK: The church is made up of every Christian person – those who believe and trust in the Lord Jesus Christ. Jesus is the builder of his church.

Nehemiah worked for King Artaxerxes of Persia (Iran) as a wine steward.

He heard news from his home-town, far off Jerusalem that the city walls were broken down and the people were in great trouble.

Nehemiah prayed to God, confessing his sin and asking for help.

When he served wine to the king, Artaxerxes noticed that Nehemiah was sad. 'What is troubling you?' he asked.

Nehemiah told the king about the state of the walls of Jerusalem. 'What do you want?' the king asked.

Nehemiah quietly prayed to God, and asked the king for permission to go back to Jerusalem to rebuild the walls.

The king was willing to let him go.

THINK: God answered Nehemiah's prayers wonderfully. When you have a problem, ask the Lord to help you. He can answer your prayers too.

Nehemiah spent the first three days in Jerusalem, surveying the damage. Lots needed to be done. Rubble had to be cleared away. The wall had to be built high and wide around the city.

Sanballat was angry when he saw Nehemiah and his helpers start to build. He said the wall would be useless. Tobiah mocked them too. 'If a fox climbed on that wall, it would fall down,' he said.

Nehemiah trusted in God and prayed for help. God answered his prayer and soon half of the huge wall was finished.

Sanballat and his wicked friends made a plot to attack the wall. Nehemiah prayed again and told the builders to carry a sword in one hand and work with the other. With God's help, the wall was finished in only fifty-two days.

Everyone, including the children, worshipped God. Ezra stood on a wooden platform and read and explained God's law to them.

The people were cheered by the words, 'The joy of the LORD is your strength.'

THINK: Joy is a gift from God, through the Lord Jesus. God is the joy of our heart when we trust in him.

Esther was a beautiful Jewish girl who lived in the land of Persia (which we call Iran today). Her cousin, Mordecai, had cared for her after her parents had died.

The King of Persia, Xerxes, held a sumptuous feast to show off his vast wealth. He ordered, Vashti, the queen, to come to entertain his guests. Vashti refused to come and King Xerxes was furious. He and his advisers decided to punish Vashti. She was the queen no longer. Someone else would be chosen to take her place.

A notice was sent through the land. All the beautiful young women were told to come to the palace. The king would choose the one he liked best.

Esther was one of the girls who came to the palace. She spent a whole year preparing to meet the king. Every day Mordecai walked past the courtyard of Esther's house, to find out if all was well.

THINK: Vashti was angry. Did you know that anger is a sin? Even when you think your anger is justified it still comes out from an evil heart and often leads to other sins. God tells his people to get rid of bitterness, rage and anger, and to be kind and forgiving. We can do this only through the power and grace of God.

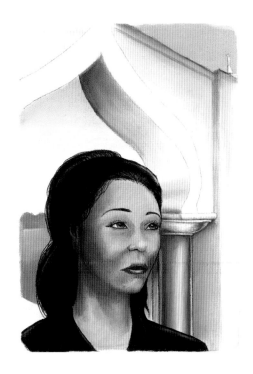

The king was pleased with Esther and chose her as queen. He made a feast in her honour. Mordecai thought it was wiser to keep the fact that Esther was a Jew a secret. Some people hated the Jews.

One day Mordecai heard two officers plotting to kill King Xerxes. He told Esther and she reported it to the king giving, Mordecai the credit. The criminals were hanged and the incident was recorded in the royal record books.

Haman was an important man on the king's staff. When he walked along the road people would bow to him – except Mordecai. Haman was so angry he decided to get rid of all the Jews, especially Mordecai.

THINK: The Bible tells us that pride like Haman's is sin. The only cure is to depend completely on Jesus Christ and give glory to him.

Wicked Haman made up a law that every Jew throughout the land would be killed on a certain day, eleven months later. The king agreed to the new law and copies of it were sent all over the country.

Mordecai was very upset. The news came to Esther too. Mordecai asked her to help save the Jews. 'How can I do that?' thought Esther. 'No one is allowed to go in to see the king without being asked.'

Mordecai urged Esther to think of something. 'Who knows, but you may have been made queen so that you could do something now.'

When Esther went to see the king three days later, he was pleased to see her and offered her anything she would like.

'I would like you and Haman to come to a banquet,' Esther replied.

They accepted. At the banquet the king again asked Esther what she wanted. Esther asked the king and Haman to come to another banquet the next day. Haman was delighted.

THINK: Isn't it amazing that we can speak to God, the King of kings at any time? We do not need to be afraid to approach him when we pray.

Even though Haman was delighted with the special honour he had been shown by Queen Esther he was still annoyed that Mordecai did not bow to him. His family suggested he get rid of Mordecai. 'Build a big gallows, and have Mordecai hanged.' What a wicked man Haman was!

God's plans overturned Haman's. That night the king could not sleep. A royal record book was read to him. The part where Mordecai saved the king was read out. The king found out that nothing had been done to honour Mordecai so he asked Haman, 'What should be done for the man the king delights to honour?'

'That must be me,' thought proud Haman. Haman suggested the man should wear royal robes and a crown and be led through the city on a horse.

'Give that honour to Mordecai, the Jew.' Haman was horrified.

THINK: Esther was afraid to tell the king her problem. We need never be afraid to tell God about any problem we have. He is a good and loving king.

The king again asked Esther at her second banquet, what he could do for her. 'O king, please spare my life, and the lives of my people.' Esther exclaimed and then she told of Haman's wicked plot.

Haman was terrified. The king was so angry he ordered that Haman should be hanged on the gallows he had built for Mordecai. Haman's land and property were given to Esther. Mordecai was made manager of the estate.

Esther begged the king to reverse the orders to kill the Jews. Another letter was quickly written, sealed with the king's ring and sent out by messengers on fast horses, mules and young camels.

The Jews were saved. Mordecai was honoured by the king. God had worked through Mordecai and Esther to save the Jews from death.

THINK: Sin can never be hidden from God. Every thought, word and deed is well known to him.

God's name is not mentioned in the book of Esther in the Bible but his love and care for his people is seen in the whole story. What we sometimes think is chance, is really God working in day to day events. This is called God's providence.

Because Esther pleased the king and was made queen, she was able to plead with him for her people. This was God's providence. Because the king could not sleep he read about Mordecai's good deeds – this also was God's providence. God is at work in our lives too. All things work together for good to those who love God.

PRAY: Thank God for how he is in charge of everything. Ask him to help you to trust in him and to trust in the fact that every moment of every day is planned by our amazing God.

Job was a rich farmer in the land of Uz. He had a family of seven sons and three daughters. God was pleased with Job. He was good and upright and respected and worshipped God.

Satan, the evil enemy of God, said, 'Job is only good because he has an easy life. Take that away and he would curse God.'

So God allowed Satan to test Job's faith. All his farm animals were either killed or stolen by raiders. A great storm struck the house where all his children were feasting. They all died.

Job was full of grief, but he still worshipped God. 'The LORD gave and the LORD has taken away. Blessed be the name of the LORD.'

Satan challenged God again. 'Job would not be so faithful if his body was suffering.' God permitted Satan to hurt Job. He had painful boils all over his body. He was miserable. Even his wife urged him to curse God.

Job refused. 'We accept good from God, should we not also accept hardship?' Job was so patient.

THINK: God is with his people in good times and in suffering. His love is so great that he gave his Son, the Lord Jesus, who died on the cross to save those who trust in him.

Job's three friends Eliphaz, Bildad and Zophar, came to comfort him. They sat for seven days and seven nights without saying a word. They were not much comfort to Job. They did not understand what had happened. One urged Job to repent, another accused him of opposing God and that he deserved his suffering. But Job still trusted in God. He responded to his friends' comments in a wise and godly way. 'I know that my Redeemer lives, and that in the end he will stand upon the earth.'

Job trusted God through all his problems. He did not blame God. He knew that trusting in God's salvation was more important than understanding his circumstances. God is bigger than any problem.

THINK: Job's friends were no comfort to him. God's Word gives great comfort to us when we are in trouble. God is described as the God of all comfort. Job mentions the name Redeemer. Jesus Christ is our Redeemer, because he died on the cross at Calvary to save his people from their sins.

Elihu gave his opinions on Job's problems. He sounded very clever but he was not helpful either. Only when God spoke did Job get a right understanding of God's power. He repented for his sinful thoughts and words.

God told Job's friends that they had spoken foolishly. Job prayed for his friends and God listened to his prayers and did not punish the friends for their foolish talk.

After Job had prayed for his friends the LORD made him prosperous again. God gave him twice as much as he had before. The LORD blessed Job greatly. He had seven more sons and three beautiful daughters. Job lived a long life after his hard experience, seeing his grandchildren and great grandchildren.

THINK: Jesus prayed for his friends and also for those who were against him. We can speak to God about anything – even about the friends that are causing us trouble.

King Solomon was very wise. God had given him this gift. Many of the wise sayings in the book of Proverbs were given by Solomon.

Solomon wrote these proverbs to teach his people how to live – how to be just and fair in dealing with others.

To be truly wise, a person must trust and honour the LORD. Wisdom is a gift from God; only a fool will not accept it. We must remember God's commands and learn and apply them to our daily lives.

If you have that wisdom from God, it does not mean that you are more clever or that you would get better marks in an exam, or even know all the answers to a Bible quiz. But we will long to know God better, to fight against sin and to live in a way that pleases him.

THINK: Jesus is even greater than Solomon. Solomon's wisdom impressed many people. We should be so amazed at what Jesus taught and what he did.

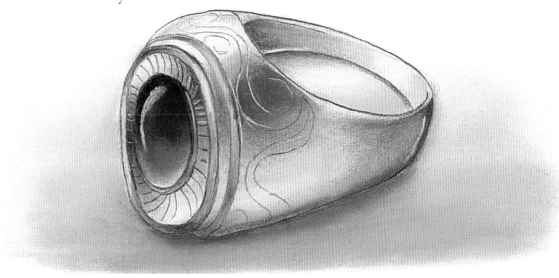

Ezekiel was called by God to be a prophet to his people living in exile in Babylon. He used visions and parables and symbols to proclaim the message of God. Much of the message was about judgement and punishment for sin. But the promise was given of the coming of the Messiah, the Lord Jesus Christ.

The last words of Ezekiel's book are 'The LORD is there.' The Hebrew words are Jehovah Shammah – the name given to the restored city of God. This is a great comfort to God's people.

Even in the most difficult times, God is there with us. 'I will never leave you or forsake you,' God has promised his people. Even when we are finding life hard or sad, it does not mean that God has forgotten us or left us. He is there helping us and making us strong.

PRAY: Thank God for the promises he makes and always keeps. Thank him for promising a Saviour. Thank him for providing Jesus, his own Son, as the Saviour of sinners.

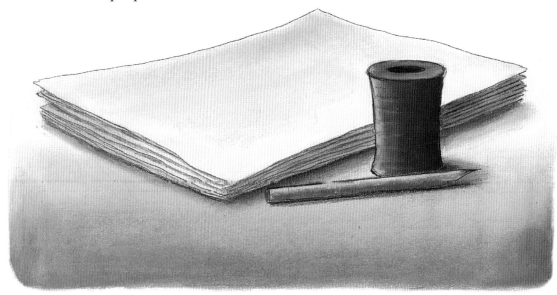

Ezekiel was given a message of hope from God in a vision. He was in a valley littered with dead, dry bones. 'Can these bones live?' the Lord asked him. 'Only you know that, Lord,' he replied.

God told him to speak to the bones. 'The Lord is going to make you live and breathe again. I will replace the flesh and muscles and cover you with skin, and breathe life into you.'

In the vision Ezekiel saw the bones coming together as skeletons, being covered with flesh and skin and breathing again.

'These represent all the people of Israel,' God told Ezekiel. 'I will breathe new life into them and they will return home again to their own land. Then at last my people will know that I am the Lord.'

THINK: The Lord Jesus gives spiritual life to his followers. He gives eternal life – life that will never end.

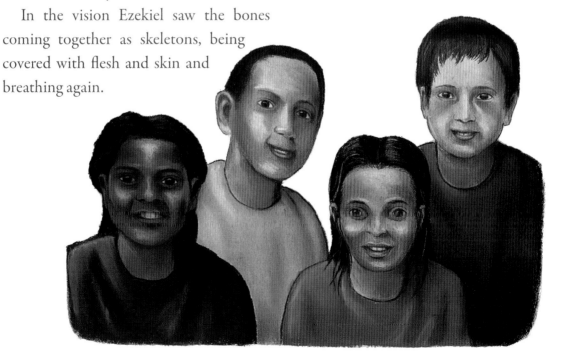

God gave Jonah an important message, 'Go to the great city of Nineveh. Tell the people there that I see their wickedness.'

Although Jonah worshipped God, he did not obey him then. Instead of going where God had told him, he headed off in the opposite direction to the port of Joppa on the Mediterranean Sea. At Joppa, Jonah found a ship ready to sail across the sea to Tarshish.

Jonah paid the fare and boarded the ship, as one of the passengers. However, no one can run away from God.

God sent a violent storm, so wild that it seemed that the ship would soon be broken up.

The sailors were scared. They threw cargo overboard to lighten the ship. They were worried. They prayed to their own false gods but of course that was no good. Only God can hear and answer prayer.

THINK: God is everywhere and can see us wherever we are, in school, at home, in an aeroplane. He still sees us when we are like Jonah, in a place where we ought not to be.

Jonah was fast asleep. The captain came down and shook him awake. 'Get up and pray to your God. Perhaps he will save us.'

'Why has this disaster happened?' one man asked. 'Let's draw lots to see who is to blame.'

So they cast lots and as it happened the lot fell on Jonah. He got the blame.

When they discovered that Jonah was running away from God, they were even more afraid.

Jonah came up with a drastic solution.

'Throw me overboard. Then the sea will be calm. This is my fault.'

The sailors did not want to do this.

They rowed harder but with no success. In desperation they cried out in prayer to the Lord God. 'O Lord, please do not let us die because of this man Jonah. Do not blame us. You, O Lord, have done just what pleases you.'

With these words they caught Jonah and threw him into the raging sea. The moment Jonah hit the water, the sea became calm. The sailors saw the power of the true God and worshipped him on the deck of the ship.

THINK: We can see God's power every day in the world around us. This should make us worship and praise him.

191. Jonah in the Big Fish - Jonah 3

Down, down went Jonah into the deep sea. But that was not the end of Jonah. God still had work for him to do.

God had arranged that a great big whale would swallow Jonah.

For three days and three nights Jonah lived inside the whale. He had air to breathe and so was saved from drowning.

Jonah was in great trouble. He cried to God in prayer from the stomach of the whale. 'I cried to God because of my trouble and he heard me. When my soul was fainting I remembered the LORD. I prayed to you. Salvation is of the LORD.'

Jonah worshipped God, confessed his wrongdoing and thanked him for his goodness in saving him. God spoke to the whale and it vomited Jonah on the dry land.

THINK: When we pray we should confess our sins to God and ask him to forgive us for our sins through the Lord Jesus Christ.

Jonah had another opportunity to obey God's voice. God said a second time, 'Go to the great city of Nineveh and preach to the people whatever I tell you.'

When he reached Nineveh he walked towards the centre, his message was clear. 'In forty days the city of Nineveh will be destroyed because of sin.'

The people of Nineveh heard Jonah's words and believed God. They were sorry for their sins. The king told everyone, 'We must all cry to God and turn from our evil ways. Perhaps God will not destroy us.'

God had mercy and did not destroy the city. Many people were changed and served the true God. But Jonah was angry because the destruction he had preached did not happen.

THINK: God's message is still the same today. 'Christ died for the ungodly. All who believe in him will be saved.'

God taught Jonah a lesson by making a large plant with big leaves to grow quickly to give Jonah shade. He then sent a worm to gnaw at the roots so the plant died. The hot wind made Jonah more and more uncomfortable.

'You are sorry that the plant was destroyed,' said God. 'Should you not have had as much pity for that great city Nineveh.'

Jonah had been shown mercy. He should have been delighted that God showed mercy to the people of Nineveh.

THINK: If we received what our sins deserve, we would all be destroyed. God tells us that the wages of sin is death. Our loving God delights to show mercy to his people. He does not give what our sins deserve. He gives the wonderful gift of eternal life, because of the Lord Jesus Christ and what he has done on the cross to take the punishment to himself that is due to us for our sin. A good prayer for us is 'God, be merciful to me, a sinner.'

Zechariah was a priest in the temple in Jerusalem. He and his wife, Elizabeth, loved the Lord God and lived holy lives. They were growing older and often prayed that God would give them a child.

One day when Zechariah was working in the temple, an angel appeared on the right side of the altar.

'Do not be afraid,' the angel said, 'Your prayer has been heard. Your wife Elizabeth shall have a son and you shall call him John.'

The angel told Zechariah that his son would bring joy to many people. Through his preaching many people would turn from their sins to love God.

Zechariah found it hard to believe the angel. The angel said, 'My name is Gabriel. God has sent me. Because you do not believe me, you will be made dumb until my words come true.'

Zechariah was unable to speak another word. He came out of the temple and was only able to make signs.

THINK: Do you believe God's Word when you hear it or read it? God's Word is completely true with no errors.

4. The Life of Jesus

Books of the Bible:

Matthew, Mark, Luke, John.

What you will read about:

Jesus' birth, Jesus' Baptism, Jesus' Early Ministry,
The Disciples, Jesus' Miracles, Jesus' Teaching,
The Parables, The Transfiguration,
The Triumphal Entry, The Crucifixion,
The Resurrection, The Ascension.

Mary was a young Jewish woman from Nazareth in Galilee. She was engaged to be married to Joseph. One day the angel Gabriel visited her. 'You are highly favoured. The LORD is with you,' he greeted her. Mary was anxious. Why was the angel speaking like this?

'Don't be afraid, Mary,' the angel said. 'God is pleased with you. You are going to have a baby boy and you will call him Jesus. He shall be a great king, the son of the Highest.'

'How can that happen to me?' Mary asked. 'I am not yet married.'

'The Holy Spirit's power shall come upon you. The holy child to whom you shall give birth will be the Son of God.'

The angel also told her, 'Your cousin, Elizabeth, is going to have a baby boy soon. Everyone thought she was too old.'

Mary believed that God would do these amazing things.

THINK: God's love is so great that he sent his Son into the world as a baby to be the Saviour of his people.

Mary went to visit her cousin Elizabeth in the hill country of Judea.

As soon as Mary entered the house, the baby inside Elizabeth moved vigorously.

Elizabeth called out loudly, 'Blessed are you among women and blessed is your child!'

God the Holy Spirit had told Elizabeth that Mary's baby was special and she believed him.

Mary praised God in a beautiful song of love to God her Saviour, 'My soul magnifies the LORD and my spirit has rejoiced in God my Saviour.'

Mary returned to Nazareth after three months. Joseph was naturally upset when he heard that Mary was expecting a baby. An angel reassured him in a dream, 'Do not be afraid to take Mary as your wife. The baby has been formed by the power of God the Holy Spirit. She will give birth to a Son and you will call his name Jesus for he shall save his people from their sins.'

THINK: We all need the Saviour. We should praise God, like Mary, for Jesus the Saviour of sinners.

Elizabeth was so happy when her baby boy was born. Her neighbours and relations were glad too when they heard how good the LORD had been to her.

When the baby was eight days old he was to be named. Some friends thought he would be called Zechariah after his father. Elizabeth said, 'Oh, no, he shall be called John.'

'None of your family is called John,' they objected. They made signs to the baby's father to see what name he wanted. Zechariah asked for something to write on, and he wrote, 'His name is John.'

Immediately Zechariah was able to speak again. The first words he spoke were words of praise to God. Zechariah told the people that the baby, John, would be a preacher one day. He would warn about sin and point people to the promised Saviour, the Lord Jesus Christ.

THINK: God loves to hear our praise. We can sing praise to him. 'It is a good thing to give thanks to the LORD, and to sing praises to your name' Psalm 92:1.

Mary and Joseph got married and lived in Nazareth. Joseph worked as a carpenter.

The ruler of the land decided that everyone had to go to their home-town to register and pay tax. Joseph belonged to the family of David so he had to go to Bethlehem. Mary had to go too.

The town of Bethlehem was busy with visitors like Mary and Joseph. There was no room for them to stay in the inn, but they were allowed to take shelter in the stable.

That night Mary's baby was born. She wrapped him in a very tight shawl, and laid him to sleep in a manger, which usually held straw for the animals.

Mary's baby was given the name Jesus which means Saviour, because he was to save his people from their sins.

THINK: Jesus was given another name, Immanuel, which means 'God with us'. Thank God that he is with us today. What an amazing blessing.

The night Jesus was born, some shepherds in the country close by, were watching over their flocks. Suddenly an angel of the Lord appeared. There was great brightness in the sky showing them the glory of the Lord. The shepherds were afraid.

'Do not be afraid,' the angel said. 'I bring you good news. Today in the city of David, the Saviour has been born. He is Christ the Lord. You will find this baby wrapped in swaddling clothes, lying in a manger.'

The angel was joined by many others and they all praised God saying, 'Glory to God in the highest, and on earth peace, good will to all men.'

When the angels returned to heaven, the shepherds said, 'Let's go to Bethlehem and see for ourselves the wonderful thing that the Lord has told us.'

They hurried to Bethlehem and found Mary and Joseph and the baby, just as the angels had said. They passed on the great news to everyone they met, praising God.

THINK: Ask God to help you to tell the good news about Jesus to the people you meet.

It was the law of the Jews, that when the first baby boy was born in a family, the mother and father had to go to the temple to make an offering to the Lord. Mary and Joseph took baby Jesus to the temple at Jerusalem where they were to offer a pair of doves or two young pigeons.

In the temple they met a good old man called Simeon. He had been told by God that he would not die until he had seen the promised Saviour.

When he saw Mary and Joseph with the baby, Simeon knew that at last he was looking at the Saviour. He took Jesus in his arms and praised the Lord. 'Now I am ready to die,' he said, 'for I have seen the Saviour of sinners.'

Joseph and Mary were amazed at what Simeon said. Simeon blessed them. 'You will have suffering too,' he told Mary.

THINK: Simeon was obeying God's Word. 'Rest in the Lord and wait patiently for him' (Ps. 37:7). God will help us to trust in him when we ask him.

There was an old lady too who met Mary and Joseph and Jesus in the temple. Her name was Anna. She was a widow, eighty-four years old. She never left the temple. All day and all night she worshipped God, fasting and praying.

When she saw baby Jesus, she too realised he was special. She came over to the family and gave thanks to God.

She spoke of Jesus to many people who were looking for the Saviour.

Anna believed that Jesus was the one promised to come and save from sin.

THINK: Anna spent a lot of time in prayer. It is good to start the day with prayer and to pray before we go to sleep at night. But we can pray at any time of the day and as often as we can.

Wise men from the East set off on a long journey to Jerusalem. They arrived at King Herod's palace. 'Where is the new-born King of the Jews?' they asked. 'We have seen his star. We want to worship him.'

Herod was angry. He summoned the chief priests and scribes. 'Where will Christ be born?' he asked. They quoted to him from the book of Micah, 'Christ will be born in Bethlehem.'

Herod passed on this information to the visitors. 'Look carefully for the young child,' he said, 'and tell me where he is so that I can go to worship him.' That was really an evil scheme.

The wise men followed the star to Bethlehem. They were guided to the house where Jesus was. The wise men fell down and worshipped Jesus. They gave him gifts of gold, frankincense and myrrh.

THINK: The wise men gave precious gifts to Jesus. Jesus wants us to give him our love and trust and obedience.

God warned the wise men to go home by a different route while an angel spoke to Joseph in a dream, 'Take the young child and his mother and go quickly to Egypt. Stay there until I tell you. Herod is trying to kill the child.'

Joseph got up in the middle of the night and set off with Mary and the baby Jesus to safety in Egypt.

Herod was very angry when he realised what the wise men had done. Herod then sent his men out to Bethlehem and the country round about, to kill all the baby boys of two years old and under. What a terrible thing to do! He thought he would be sure to get rid of the Messiah that way. But Jesus was safe in Egypt.

After Herod died, the angel of the Lord again spoke to Joseph in a dream, telling him it was safe to go back to Israel. They settled in Nazareth where Joseph worked as a carpenter.

THINK: Remember that Jesus grew up just like other children, but he had no sin. He obeyed God's law perfectly.

Every year Mary and Joseph went to Jerusalem to attend the Passover Feast. They took Jesus for the first time when he was twelve years old. When they were going home from the feast, Jesus stayed behind in the temple. His parents thought he was in the company of friends on the way home to Nazareth.

When they discovered he was not in the company they hurried back to Jerusalem. After three days searching, they found him in the temple, sitting with the teachers, listening to them and asking questions. Everyone was astonished at his understanding and at the answers he gave.

'Why did you do this?' Mary asked. 'Your father and I have been very worried looking for you.'

'Did you not know,' replied Jesus, 'that I have to do my Father's business?' Jesus was speaking about his heavenly Father, God.

THINK: Mary often thought about what Jesus had said. Try to think about Jesus' words that you read in the Bible. Ask him to help you to remember.

John lived a simple life in the desert land of Judea. His clothes were made of camel's hair and he wore a leather belt. His food was locusts and wild honey. His work was very important.

He preached to the crowds, 'Turn from your sins. Believe the gospel. The Kingdom of God is near.'

Many people from Judea and Jerusalem were baptised by John in the River Jordan. They confessed their sins and were made willing to turn from their sin to God. Being baptised in the water was an outward symbol of having their sins washed away.

The religious leaders wondered who John was. 'I am not the Christ,' he told them. 'I am just a voice crying in the wilderness. The man coming after me is much more important.

'I am not worthy to stoop down and undo his sandals. I baptise with water, but he will baptise you with the Holy Spirit.'

THINK: John's message is for us too. We also must turn from our sin and believe the good news of the gospel that Jesus died to give us eternal life.

One day Jesus came to the River Jordan to see John. He asked John to baptise him. John was surprised. 'I need to be baptised by you,' he said, 'and yet you are coming to me.'

Jesus had no sin so his baptism did not mean having his sins washed away. He was baptised as an example to us, and to show us that although he was God, he was also fully man.

When Jesus came up out of the water of the River Jordan, the heavens opened up and the Spirit of God came down on him, in the form of a dove. God the Father's voice was heard from heaven, saying, 'This is my beloved Son in whom I am well pleased.' God was pleased with what Jesus had done.

John always gave the most important place to Jesus. His preaching always pointed to him. 'I must become less important,' he said. 'Jesus must become greater.'

THINK: The Bible tells us that there is only one God. However, this story tells of three different persons in this one God – God the Father, God the Son and God the Holy Spirit.

When John saw Jesus coming towards him, he said to the crowd, 'Look, the Lamb of God who takes away the sin of the world.'

What did he mean? A lamb was used as a sacrifice for sin in the temple worship.

John the Baptist realised that Jesus had come to save his people from their sins.

When Isaac asked his father where the lamb for the sacrifice was (see story 20), Abraham said that God would provide a lamb. That day they found a ram to offer as a sacrifice. Abraham did not have to offer his son. Isaac's question was answered in Jesus, the Lamb of God.

John pointed Jesus out to his congregation and to his disciples.

PRAY: Thank God that he did sacrifice his own Son for sin. Because he did, his people can have sins taken away and enjoy eternal life with God.

For forty days after his baptism, Jesus was alone in the desert. He was tired and hungry. Satan spoke to him, tempting him to do wrong.

'If you are the Son of God, make these stones into bread,' he said. Jesus knew the Bible well. He quoted from the Bible in reply, 'It is written: man shall not live by bread alone, but by every word that God says.'

The devil tried again. He took Jesus up to one of the high towers of the temple. 'If you are the Son of God, throw yourself to the ground. God will send an angel to take care of you.' Again Jesus used the Bible, 'It is written,' he said, 'You shall not tempt the Lord your God.'

Once more the devil tried to make Jesus sin. Up on a high mountain he said, 'I will give you all these lands to you if you just bow down and worship me.'

'Go away, Satan,' Jesus said, 'It is written, You shall worship the Lord your God and serve only him.'

The devil then gave up. Angels came to attend to Jesus who had used God's Word to resist the devil.

THINK: When we are tempted to sin, reading and thinking about Jesus and what he has done, will help us to resist.

Andrew was a fisherman on the Sea of Galilee. He was a follower of John the Baptist. When Jesus passed by, John said, 'Look, the Lamb of God.' Andrew realised that Jesus was the Christ, the Saviour of sinners. Andrew hurried to find his brother, Simon. 'We have found the Saviour,' he said. He took Simon to meet Jesus.

Jesus spoke kindly to Simon and gave him another name. He called him Peter which means 'a rock.'

'Come and follow me,' Jesus said to Andrew and Peter, 'and I will make you fishers of men.' They immediately left their fishing nets and followed Jesus. They were his first disciples.

A little further on he met two other fishermen, James and his brother, John. They were mending their nets in their boat. When Jesus called them, they left their father, Zebedee, in the boat with the hired servants and followed Jesus.

THINK: We can meet Jesus when we hear about him in his Word. We follow him when we obey his Word.

The next day Jesus chose two more disciples. One was called Philip. 'Follow me,' he said to him.

Philip found his friend, Nathanael. 'We have found the man that Moses and the prophets spoke about,' Philip exclaimed, 'Jesus of Nazareth, the Son of Joseph.'

'Can any good thing come out of Nazareth?' asked Nathanael.

'Come and see for yourself,' replied Philip.

When Jesus saw Nathanael coming towards him, he said, 'Here comes an honest man – a true son of Israel.'

'How do you know what I am like?' demanded Nathanael.

'I saw you under the fig tree, before Philip called you,' Jesus replied.

'You are the Son of God,' admitted Nathanael, 'the king of Israel.'

Nathanael became a disciple too.

In all, Jesus had twelve special followers called disciples.

THINK: A disciple, or Christian, has faith and trust in the Lord Jesus and obeys his Word.

One day Jesus saw Matthew sitting working in his tax collector's booth. Nobody liked the tax collectors, they worked for the Romans who had taken control of the land.

'Follow me,' Jesus said to Matthew. He left his work and followed Jesus immediately.

Matthew invited Jesus and his disciples to have dinner at his house. Many of Matthew's friends came too.

When the Jewish teachers, the Pharisees, saw Jesus at the dinner party they were shocked.

'Why does your teacher, Jesus, eat with tax collectors and sinners?' they asked the disciples.

Jesus overheard them, 'I have come to help sinners,' he said, 'not people who think they are good. Healthy people do not need a doctor, sick people do.'

Matthew became one of Jesus' special followers.

THINK: Jesus still shows mercy to sinners who follow and trust in him. Trust in him.

Jesus and his disciples and his mother, Mary, were all invited to a wedding in Cana in Galilee. During the feast the servants discovered that the wine was finished. How embarrassing for the hosts.

Mary came to Jesus and told him about the problem. 'What can I do?' he said. 'My time has not yet come.'

Mary said to the servants, 'Do whatever he tells you.'

'Fill these big stone water pots with water,' Jesus told them. 'Now draw out some and take it to the man in charge of the feast.'

The man tasted it and called to the bridegroom, 'This is really good wine.'

'Most people give the best wine first,' he said, 'and then bring out the poorer, but you have kept the good wine until now.'

The servants who filled the water pots and drew the wine, knew that a miracle had been performed that day. This was the first miracle that Jesus did.

THINK: Jesus is God the Son and so the Creator of all things. He has power over all his creation.

One night a Pharisee called Nicodemus came to Jesus. He knew that Jesus was a teacher sent from God. Jesus said to him, 'No one can see the kingdom of God unless he is born again.' Nicodemus could not understand that. 'How can you be born again when you are old?' he asked.

Jesus explained, 'This is not a natural birth but a spiritual birth.' Jesus compared the spiritual birth to the wind. We cannot see it but we can see the effects of the wind and hear it. We cannot see spiritual birth but it is possible to see the effects of it in a person's life.

Nicodemus was a clever man, but he was puzzled. Jesus continued to tell the good news of the gospel. 'God so loved the world that he gave his one and only Son (Jesus Christ) that whoever believes in him shall not perish but have eternal life.'

PRAY: Thank God for his most wonderful gift – his own dear Son sent to this world to be the Saviour of sinners.

Jesus was travelling to Galilee through Samaria. At noon he sat down by a well, tired and thirsty, while his disciples went into town to buy food. A Samaritan woman came to draw water from the well. Jesus asked her for a drink. This surprised her because Jews didn't usually speak to Samaritans.

Jesus said, 'If you knew who was asking you for a drink, you would be asking me for a drink. I can offer you living water.'

The woman wondered what he would draw the water with and asked, 'Where can you get this living water?'

Jesus answered, 'Everyone who drinks from this well will be thirsty again. But whoever drinks the water I will give will never thirst.'

The woman asked Jesus to give her this water. 'I'll never have to come to the well again!' she exclaimed.

THINK; The woman didn't understand what Jesus meant. The water he spoke about was special water to satisfy the soul. Jesus offers the water of everlasting life to us too. We are truly satisfied when we believe in him.

When the woman said to Jesus, 'Give me this water so that I don't have to keep coming to the well,' Jesus began to explain to her what this water really was. 'Call your husband and come back,' Jesus said.

'I have no husband,' she replied.

Jesus knew that this was true. She had had five husbands and was now living with a man who was not her husband. The woman realised that Jesus was a prophet. She wanted to speak about religious differences between Jews and Samaritans but Jesus directed her mind to the true worship of God. He showed her that he was the promised Messiah, the Son of God. She believed in Jesus, left her water pot at the well and ran to tell everyone, 'Come and see a man who knows all about me. Is not this the Christ?' she exclaimed.

PRAY: Ask God to help you to share what you know about Jesus with others.

Jesus started to preach when he was about thirty years old. One day Jesus preached an amazing sermon as he was sitting on a mountainside with his disciples. It is full of good advice about how to live. Jesus taught about the importance of love. It is not enough to love only those who are good to us. Jesus tells us to love those who are our enemies.

'Do not worry about where you will get enough food and clothes,' says Jesus. 'You are of more value than the birds and God feeds them. The fields are covered with colourful flowers, more beautiful than even Solomon's clothes'. God our Father knows what we need.

Jesus tells us to give generously to God and to the poor without drawing attention to our good deeds. God will reward openly those who give in secret.

THINK: It is easy to love those who love us. God shows his love and care for good people and bad. He gives the sunshine and the rain to both. We should be like God in heaven and show love and care for those who do not show love to us.

In the Sermon on the Mount, Jesus gave a list of those who are blessed or truly happy – not the clever, or rich or famous – quite a different list.

Blessed are the poor in spirit, those who mourn, the meek, those who hunger and thirst for righteousness, the merciful, the pure in heart, the peacemakers, those who are persecuted for righteousness.

These people are blessed with spiritual blessings – the kingdom of heaven, the comfort and provision of God and the joy of belonging to God.

Even suffering for the sake of Jesus is a great blessing. 'Rejoice,' Jesus says, 'if people hurt you or tell lies about you for my sake. Your reward will be great in heaven.'

PRAY: Ask the Lord God that you will know these special blessings from him and value them.

Jesus taught us about prayer. We should pray in a quiet secret place, not trying to show off to other people. God knows what we need but he wants us to pray to him. If a little boy asked his father for bread, would he give him a stone? Of course not. If the boy asked for a fish, the father would never give him a serpent. So God in heaven gives good things to his children who pray to him.

Jesus gave a lovely example of a prayer.

Our Father in heaven, hallowed be your name, your kingdom come, your will be done on earth as it is in heaven.

Give us today our daily bread. Forgive us all our sins as we also have forgiven those who sin against us.

And lead us not into temptation but deliver us from the evil one.

For yours is the Kingdom, and the power and the glory, for ever. Amen.

THINK: It is a good idea to learn this prayer off by heart as it is a prayer that was taught by the Lord Jesus himself.

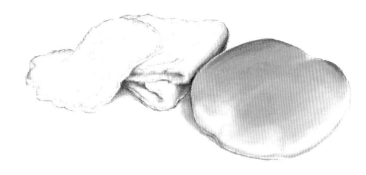

Jesus was teaching a big crowd on the shore of the Sea of Galilee. Two fishing boats were moored close to the shore. The fishermen were washing their nets close by. Jesus climbed into Peter's boat and asked him to push it out a little from the shore. From the boat he preached to the people on the shore.

When he had finished speaking, he asked Peter to throw out his fishing nets over the side to catch some fish. 'We have been working hard all night fishing,' Peter replied, 'and haven't caught a thing. But because you say so, I will let down the nets.'

The nets filled with so many fish that they began to break. They called to their partners, James and John, in the other boat to help. Both boats were full of fish.

Peter knelt before Jesus, 'I am a sinful man. You are the Lord.'

'Don't be afraid,' Jesus answered Peter.

Peter, Andrew, James and John left their boats and nets and followed Jesus.

THINK: Jesus had power over all creation, even the fish. Thank him for his care over everything in your life.

Four men decided to take their paralysed friend to Jesus for help. He could not walk so they carried him on a mat.

Jesus was teaching in a house nearby. Crowds of people filled the house. The friends could not get near Jesus. So they climbed up from the outside stairs to the roof, made an opening and lowered their friend down through the roof, right in front of Jesus.

When Jesus saw the men's faith, he said to their friend, 'Your sins are forgiven.' Some of the listeners were indignant at this. To prove that he had power to forgive sin, Jesus said to the man, 'Get up and walk. Take your mat and go home.'

Immediately, he jumped up and walked home, praising God. Everyone who saw Jesus' wonderful power, was amazed, and gave praise to God.

THINK: When we pray for our friends and family, we are bringing them to Jesus.

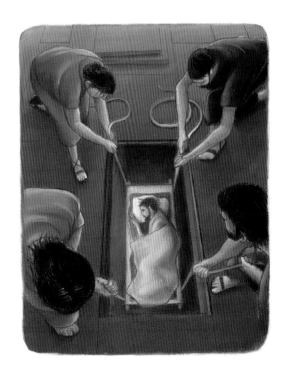

Some Jewish elders came to Jesus in Capernaum. 'An important Roman soldier, who is in charge of a hundred men, needs your help. His servant is very sick and is about to die.' This soldier had been very helpful to the Jewish people. Jesus agreed to go to the soldier's home.

But not far from the house, some friends came to meet Jesus. 'Lord, do not go to any trouble. Our friend, the Roman soldier, does not feel worthy to have you in his house. But he believes that if you just say the word, his servant will be healed.' The soldier was a man of authority, used to giving orders. He believed that Jesus was a man of authority too. He had the authority and power of God.

Jesus was amazed at the soldier's faith. The friends went back to the house and found that the servant was completely better.

THINK: Faith is a gift from God, when we trust in Jesus Christ only for salvation.

Jairus was an important ruler in the Jewish church. His twelve-year-old daughter became very ill. Jairus was so anxious. He was afraid she would die. Jairus went to Jesus for help. 'Please come to my house. My daughter is so ill. Please help her,' he begged.

Jesus made his way to Jairus' house. The crowds pressing round made it difficult to get through. Jesus was detained further helping a sick lady.

As Jairus was waiting for Jesus, some one came from his house. 'Your daughter is dead,' he said, 'do not trouble the Master.'

When Jesus heard this, he said, 'Don't be afraid. Just believe and she will be made better.'

Crowds of people were weeping outside the house. Jesus went in with Jairus and his wife, and Peter, James and John. He took the little girl's hand and said, 'Little girl, get up.'

Immediately, she got out of bed. Her mother and father were overjoyed.

'Give her something to eat now,' Jesus ordered.

THINK: Jairus knew that he could go to Jesus for help. We too can go to Jesus with any problem and ask him to help us.

223. The Woman with the Issue of Blood - Luke 8, Matthew 9

On the way to Jairus' house, Jesus suddenly stopped and asked, 'Who touched me?' Answers came from all around. 'It wasn't me!' 'No, I did not touch you.' 'Not me either.'

Peter said to Jesus, 'The crowd is so close. It is not surprising that someone has touched you.'

Then a woman came out of the crowd. She was afraid and trembling. She fell down in front of Jesus and told her story. 'I have been ill for twelve years with internal bleeding. I have spent all my money on doctor's bills but not one of them could help me. When I saw you, Jesus, I thought that if I could only touch the hem of your garment, I might be healed. As soon as I touched, I was healed.'

Jesus comforted and encouraged the woman, 'You have been healed because of your faith in me. Go in peace.'

THINK: The woman's faith was weak and small. But her faith was in the right person – the Lord Jesus. We should trust in Jesus Christ, the Saviour too.

One Sabbath day, Peter went to the synagogue in Capernaum. Jesus was preaching that day. After the service, Peter invited Jesus to his house.

In the house, Peter's wife's mother was very ill in bed, with a bad fever. The family was very worried.

'Can you do anything to help her?' they asked Jesus.

Jesus went to her bedside and touched her hand. She became better right away. The fever was completely gone and she felt quite cool.

She felt so well that she got up at once to give food to Jesus and Peter and the others.

That evening as the sun was setting, many sick people were brought to Jesus. He placed his hands on each one, and he healed them.

THINK: The Lord Jesus showed his power over disease and disability. All healing comes from God.

Jesus and his disciples set out to sail across the Sea of Galilee. While they were crossing the lake, Jesus fell asleep in the boat because he was tired.

Soon a great storm blew up, the wind howled, the waves came right over the sides of the boat.

The disciples became more and more frightened even though Jesus was in the boat with them. They woke Jesus up. 'Lord, save us!' they shouted, 'We are going to drown.'

Jesus said to them, 'Why are you so afraid? How weak your faith is.' Jesus then spoke to the wind and the sea saying, 'Peace, be still.'

The wind stopped blowing. The sea became calm. The disciples were astonished at Jesus' power over the wind and sea.

THINK: God's powerful Word made the sea. Jesus, the Son of God, used his powerful Word to calm the sea.

Jesus met a man as he got off the boat on the other side of the lake from Galilee. This man had been possessed by an evil spirit for a long time. This made him act strangely. People tried to chain him but he simply broke the chains and rushed out to the desert.

When this man saw Jesus, he shrieked and fell to the ground screaming. He knew he was the Son of God most high.

Jesus commanded the demons to leave him. There was a herd of pigs feeding nearby. The demons left the poor man and entered into the pigs. The whole herd rushed down the hillside into the lake below where they drowned.

When the news reached the town, people came out to see what had happened. They were not pleased when they saw what happened to their livestock. But the man who had been possessed by an evil spirit was now sitting quietly at Jesus' feet, clothed properly and in his right mind.

'Go and tell your family about the wonderful things God has done for you,' Jesus told him.

THINK: The man's life was completely changed because Jesus has all authority. He has more power than any evil demon.

After a busy day, Jesus told his disciples to sail back across the Sea of Galilee. Jesus wanted time alone to pray to God his Father.

As the disciples were rowing it became dark. The wind blew strongly against them. The sea was rough and the little boat was tossed about by the waves. Out of the darkness the disciples saw someone walking on the waves. They were terrified. 'It's a ghost!' one of them said.

Then they heard the voice of Jesus saying, 'It is I. Do not be afraid.'

Peter shouted back, 'Lord, if it is you, tell me to walk on the water to meet you.'

'Come,' replied Jesus. Peter climbed over the side of the boat and began to walk on the water towards Jesus. But when Peter looked at the tossing waves he became afraid. He began to sink. 'Lord, save me!' he shouted.

Jesus reached out his hand and caught Peter. The wind died down when they climbed into the boat.

THINK: We get into trouble too when we take our attention away from the Lord Jesus and focus on our problems.

One day Jesus asked his disciples, 'Who do people say I am?'

'Some say you are John the Baptist,' they answered, 'and some say Elijah, and some say Jeremiah or one of the prophets.'

'And who do you say I am?' Jesus asked them.

Peter was the first to reply. 'You are the Christ, the Son of the living God,' he said.

Peter was right and Jesus said to him, 'It is my Father in heaven who has taught you that.'

What would your answer be if Jesus were to ask you the question, 'Who do you say that I am?' He is not just a good man, or a great teacher. Just as God taught Peter the right answer, so he can teach you. Jesus is the Christ, the Son of the living God.

PRAY: We need to see our need of a Saviour and realise what a great Saviour Jesus is.

One day in Capernaum, Peter saw the temple money collectors coming towards him.

They asked him, 'Does your Master pay money for the work of the temple?'

'Yes,' said Peter.

Peter went to tell Jesus about the money collectors. When they met, Jesus spoke first, for he knew what Peter was going to say.

'What do you think?' Jesus asked Peter. 'Would a king take tax money from his own children or from strangers?'

'From strangers,' Peter replied.

Jesus said to him, 'Then the children are free.'

Jesus meant that he was the Son of God and did not need to pay money for his Father's house, the temple.

But he did not want to offend so he said he would pay the money.

Jesus told Peter, 'Go down to the shore and throw a fishing hook into the sea and take up the first fish you catch. When you open its mouth you will find a coin which will pay the temple money for both of us.'

THINK: Jesus has power over all nature – his creation. Even the fish in the sea are under his control.

Jesus told this story to a crowd of people. A farmer went out to his field to sow some seed. He walked up and down, scattering seed to the left and right. Some seed fell on the pathway. However, the birds soon came and gobbled up the seed.

Some seed fell on shallow, stony ground. These seeds grew quickly and soon green shoots showed through the earth. But when the sun shone brightly and the day became hot, these shoots withered and died, because their roots could not reach down to get moisture.

Other seeds fell among the thorns and weeds. These seeds grew but the thorns grew too and soon choked the good corn.

Some seeds landed on good ground, with no stones or thorns or weeds. This seed grew well and eventually the farmer would harvest his corn – reaping, perhaps, thirty times as much as he had sown or even sixty times or even a hundred times as much.

THINK: Jesus taught the people when he preached to them. He teaches us too when he speaks to us through his Word, the Bible.

Not everyone understood the meaning of the story that Jesus told about the farmer sowing the seed. Jesus explained the story or parable to his disciples.

The seed is like the Word of God. God sends his Word in different ways to men and women, boys and girls.

Some people hear God's Word but very soon the devil makes them think of something else and they forget about the Bible. That is like the seed that fell on the pathway, stolen away by the birds.

Other people hear God's Word and listen to it gladly. When trouble comes or if someone laughs at them, their interest in God's Word withers like the seed on the stony ground.

There are people who hear God's Word but riches and pleasures are more important to them and any interest in the Bible is choked, like the seed sown among thorns.

But there are some people who hear God's Word, love it and obey it. Their lives are made new. Their lives are fruitful like the seed sown on good ground.

PRAY: Ask God to help you to be like the good ground and to love God's Word and obey it.

John the Baptist preached against the sins of the people, telling them to repent and turn to God. He even warned King Herod about his sin. He had married Herodias, his brother's wife, which was against God's law. Herod was not sorry for his sin. He and Herodias were very angry with John.

Herod locked John up in prison. John heard news about the work Jesus was doing. He sent two of his friends to Jesus with a question, 'Are you the one that has come from God, or should we look for another man?'

Jesus sent back a reply. 'Tell John about what you have seen and heard. The blind can see, the lame can walk, the lepers are cleansed and the deaf hear, the dead are raised to life and the poor have the gospel preached to them.'

This reassured John that Jesus was indeed the Son of God.

THINK: Jesus is truly a man and also truly God. He became man so that he could take the punishment for the sin of all his people.

A man with a withered, useless hand met Jesus in the synagogue one Sabbath day. Some religious leaders, called Pharisees, wanted to find an excuse to accuse Jesus of wrongdoing.

'Is it lawful to heal on the Sabbath?' they asked. Jesus knew it was right to do good things on the Sabbath. 'If any of you had a sheep that fell into a pit on the Sabbath, would you not pull it out? How much more valuable is a man than a sheep!'

He said to the man, 'Stretch out your hand.'

The man found he could do that. His hand was strong again.

The Pharisees were so angry. They even plotted how they might kill Jesus.

THINK: Jesus is the perfect Son of God. He kept the law perfectly. Those who accused him did not understand God's ways.

King Herod had a big party on his birthday. He invited all the important men in the land. Herodias' daughter danced for Herod. He and his guests were so pleased with her that Herod said, 'I will give you anything you ask for, even half of my kingdom.'

She did not ask for jewels, or horses or a palace. After speaking with her mother, the girl came back to Herod. 'Give me John the Baptist's head on a big plate!'

King Herod was very upset by this request, but he did not want to back down on his promise. He sent the dreadful command to the prison to have John beheaded. His head was brought to the palace on a big plate and presented to the young dancer who brought it to her mother.

John's friends took his body from the prison and buried it. Then they went to find Jesus and told him all that had happened.

THINK: When you are sad or have a problem, the best thing to do is to tell Jesus. He is our best friend.

235. Five Thousand Fed - Matthew 14, John 9

Jesus and his disciples sailed across the lake to find a quiet place to rest. But large crowds made their way on foot round the lake to reach the place where Jesus was. When Jesus saw them, he took pity on them and healed many sick people.

In the evening the disciples asked Jesus to send the people home. 'Can you not give them something to eat?' he asked.

There was a boy in the crowd who had five small loaves and two fish. That was all the food they could find. The disciples wondered how that could feed 5,000 people. Jesus told his disciples to make all the people sit down in groups on the grass. He then took the loaves and the fish and gave thanks to God.

Jesus broke the loaves and fish into pieces and handed them to the disciples who gave the food out to all the people. Jesus who is the creator of all things multiplied the food to feed over 5,000 people.

Afterwards, the disciples gathered up twelve baskets full of leftover food. Jesus had provided more than enough.

THINK: Jesus called himself the 'Bread of Life'. He satisfies the longing of the hungry soul.

One day Jesus took Peter, James and John up a high mountain to pray.

While they were watching, Jesus changed. His face shone as brightly as the sun. His clothes became as white as light. They also saw Moses and Elijah talking with Jesus about his death which would soon happen in Jerusalem. Peter, James and John felt sleepy but soon became wide awake when they saw Jesus in all his glory.

Then a bright cloud covered them and they heard God's voice saying about Jesus, 'This is my beloved Son in whom I am well pleased. Hear him.'

Peter and the others were so afraid that they fell to the ground. Jesus came over to them and touched them. When they looked round, they saw that Jesus was alone.

THINK: Jesus is worthy of our worship. God is pleased with him. We should be too.

Mary and her sister, Martha, lived with their brother, Lazarus in the town of Bethany. They were friends of Jesus. Sometimes he went to their house for a meal.

One suppertime Martha was very anxious that everything would be right for her guest, Jesus. While she was busy cooking and preparing the meal, her sister, Mary, was sitting quietly beside Jesus listening to all his wise words and good advice.

Martha was tired and cross. 'Why don't you tell Mary to help me, Lord?' she demanded. 'Don't you care that she has left me to do all the work alone?'

'Martha, Martha,' Jesus lovingly replied, 'you are anxious and bothered about all your work. There is one thing that is most important. Mary is doing the right thing. What she has chosen will do her good always.'

THINK: Jesus speaks to us in his Word, the Bible. It is good for us to take time to listen to him like Mary did.

One day the sisters, Mary and Martha, were very worried. Lazarus, their brother, was very ill.

'What can we do?' they wondered. 'Let's send for Jesus to come.' They sent a message to Jesus telling him that Lazarus was ill.

Jesus did not immediately rush to Bethany. This was not because he did not care but because he had a much greater miracle to work in Lazarus' life. Jesus stayed where he was, teaching and healing people.

Two days later he set off for Lazarus' home in Bethany. 'I want to go to waken our friend, Lazarus. He is sleeping.' The disciples did not understand what he meant. Jesus told them plainly. 'Lazarus is dead. I am glad that I was not there, for your sakes. When you see what I will do, you will believe in me. Let's go to him now.'

THINK: Jesus knows everything. His timing is always right. We can be impatient, but the Lord will do everything well and at the right time.

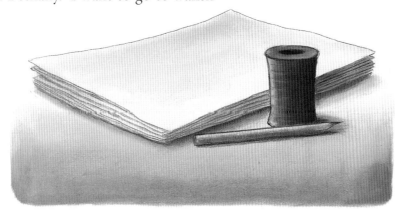

When Martha heard that Jesus was on his way to see them, she ran along the road to meet him. Lazarus had been dead and buried for four days.

'If only you had been here,' she cried, 'Lazarus would not have died.'

'Your brother will rise again,' Jesus assured her.

'I know he will rise again in the resurrection on the last day,' she replied.

'I am the resurrection and the life. Whoever believes in me shall live and never die,' replied Jesus.

'I believe you are the Christ, the Son of God who came into the world,' Martha confessed.

Mary came to see Jesus too. Jesus was sad to see Mary so upset and the family's friends weeping. Jesus wept too.

At Lazarus' grave he said, 'Roll back the stone.'

He shouted, 'Lazarus, come out!'

Lazarus walked out, wrapped in the grave clothes. What a joy for Mary and Martha to take Lazarus home again.

THINK: If you believe that Jesus is the Son of God and that in him alone is life, you too will receive eternal life and be in heaven with God, at last.

Six days before the Passover, Jesus came again to Bethany. A dinner was given in his honour. Lazarus sat at the table with Jesus while Martha was busy serving the meal.

Mary came into the room with a very expensive jar of perfumed ointment. She poured all of the ointment over Jesus' feet and then wiped his feet with her hair. She did this to show Jesus how much she loved him. She gave him the most precious possession she had.

Judas, the disciple who later betrayed Jesus, complained at this great waste. 'This ointment could have been sold, and the money given to the poor,' he grumbled.

Jesus was pleased with Mary's loving action. He did not think it was a waste. He knew that he would soon die.

'Mary has anointed my body now, he said, 'for my burial.'

THINK: If we love Jesus we should want to live for him and give him our time and energy and everything that is precious to us.

A king prepared a wonderful wedding feast for his son. The invitations were sent out but when everything was ready, the guests refused to come.

'I am too busy. I must attend to my farm. Please excuse me,' said one.

'I need to see to my business,' said another.

Some were not so polite. They grabbed the servants who had brought the invitation and beat them up and murdered them.

The king was angry. He sent out his soldiers to punish these ungrateful people.

'We will find other guests,' he said. 'Go out into the streets and invite any poor person you find.'

The feast had plenty of guests.

Jesus told this story as a picture of God the Father asking sinners to believe in his Son, Jesus, and to share the blessings he has provided.

THINK: Jesus still invites sinners. to come to him. Are you responding to his invitation, 'Come to me'?

God's Word tells us to love God with all our heart, soul, strength and mind and also to love our neighbour as ourselves. 'Who is my neighbour?' a lawyer asked Jesus one day. Jesus told a story to explain.

A man travelled on a dangerous road from Jerusalem to Jericho. He was attacked by thieves who left him beaten up by the roadside. A priest came along, saw the man and hurried on as fast as he could. Another religious man, a Levite, came next. He did not help either.

The next person to see the poor man was a Samaritan. Jews and Samaritans did not normally speak to each other, but this man took pity on the injured man, gave him first aid and then took him on his donkey to a nearby inn. He looked after him that night. The next day the Samaritan gave money to the innkeeper to look after the man until he was well enough to travel. Any extra costs he would repay the next time he was passing.

'Which person was the neighbour to the injured man?' Jesus asked. 'The Samaritan who was kind,' was the reply. 'You should do the same,' said Jesus.

THINK: Jesus told this story to help us understand that God wants us to love our neighbour as ourselves and also to love God with all our heart.

Thousands of people gathered round to listen to Jesus' teaching. He spoke particularly to his disciples. 'Do not be afraid of anyone who might try to kill you, rather fear God. Are not five sparrows sold for two pence, yet not one of them is forgotten by God? You are much more valuable than many sparrows. Every hair on your head is counted by God.'

'Don't worry about what you have to wear or to eat. Life is about more than food and clothes. The birds don't have storehouses or barns yet God feeds each one of them.

'The lilies don't work, yet not even King Solomon was dressed so beautifully as a grass field with flowers. Do not worry about these things.'

THINK: It is much more important to belong to the Kingdom of God than to have lots of riches. All who love and trust Jesus belong to his kingdom. Jesus is the king.

The religious leaders, the Pharisees, complained when Jesus made friends with tax collectors and sinners. But those people were important to Jesus. He told a story to explain.

If a man has one hundred sheep and one gets lost, what will he do? He will leave the other ninety-nine sheep safely grazing and search for the lost sheep. He will not give up until he finds it. How happy he will be carrying home the stray sheep on his shoulders. This newly found sheep will be a cause for celebration. Friends and neighbours will join in.

In the same way there is joy in heaven each time Jesus finds a sinner and brings him home to himself. Jesus does not want anyone to be lost.

THINK: Do you realise that without Jesus as your saviour you are lost in your sin?

Jesus told the story of a woman who had ten precious silver coins. One day one of the coins was missing. She was determined to find it.

She lit a lamp to brighten up the room, fetched her brush and began to sweep every corner of the house. She swept and swept until at last she caught sight of the missing coin in a corner.

How pleased she was. She shouted to her friends and neighbours, 'I have found my lost coin!' Her friends were so happy for her.

Jesus then said, 'This is what it is like in heaven when a sinner who was lost, repents and turns back to God.'

THINK: Jesus, the Son of God, came to this world, to seek for lost people and to save them from their sins. Have you trusted in Jesus for yourself?

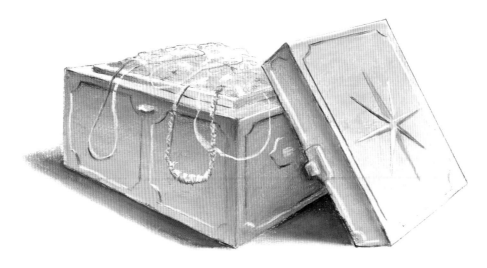

Jesus told a story about a father who had two sons. The older worked on his father's farm. The younger son wanted to leave home and see the world. So he asked his father if he could have his share of the family money. His father agreed. The younger son left home. He went to live in a foreign country and quickly spent all his father's money on wild parties and bad company.

Then famine came to the land. The young man was now without money or food. He had to get work looking after pigs. He felt so hungry that he could have eaten the pigs' food.

Then he started to think, 'Here I am starving to death, while my father's servants have plenty to eat. I will go back to my father's house and admit that I have sinned against him and against God. I will ask if I can become one of his servants.'

THINK: We turn our back on God the Heavenly Father when we disobey or ignore his Word. It is good to realise our great need of God the Lord and to repent and ask for forgiveness.

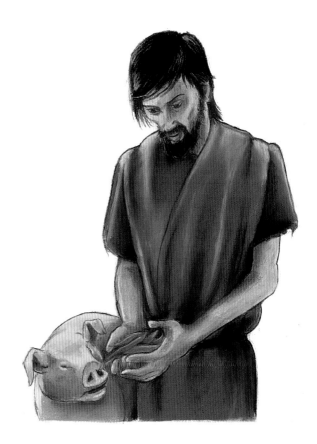

The lost son started off for home. His father saw him coming from a distance. He ran towards him and welcomed him with open arms.

The young son confessed that he had done wrong. 'I am no longer worthy to be called your son,' he said.

But his father ordered his servants to bring out special clothes and prepare a special meal. 'My son was dead, but now is alive. He was lost and is found.'

The older son came in from work, and asked what was happening. When he learned of the celebration for his brother, he was jealous. 'I have been slaving for you for years and never disobeyed you, yet you never gave a party for me and my friends.'

His father gently replied, 'My son, everything I have is yours. It is right for us to be joyful because the son I thought was dead is alive. He was lost and is now found.'

THINK: The loving, forgiving father shows us a picture of the loving and forgiving God. We love him because he first loved us.

Ten men met Jesus, as he was going into a village. They all had a skin disease called leprosy. It was very infectious. They were not allowed to go near anyone, not even their families.

They stood at a distance and called out loudly to Jesus, 'Jesus, have mercy on us,' they begged.

Jesus healed them all. They had to go to the priest, who would confirm that they were well, and could go back to their homes.

Only one man, a Samaritan, came back to Jesus to say, 'Thank you.' He praised God with a loud voice and threw himself down at Jesus' feet.

'Where are the other nine men?' Jesus asked. 'Only this foreigner has come back to give praise to God.'

'Get up and go home,' Jesus told the Samaritan man, 'your faith has made you well.'

PRAY: Ask God the Father to give you the gift of faith so that you will believe all that is said in the Bible about the Lord Jesus, the Saviour, and so that you will trust in him.

Jesus told a parable to those who were proud of their good deeds and looked down on others.

Two men went to the temple to pray. One was a Pharisee and the other a tax collector. The Pharisee was proud of himself and thought he was very good. When he prayed, he prayed about himself.

'God, I thank you that I am not greedy, dishonest and immoral like other people. I am not like that tax collector. I fast twice a week and give a tenth of my money to you.' He was very smug.

The tax collector was different. He knew he was a sinner. He bowed his head and prayed, 'God, have mercy on me a sinner.'

Jesus then explained that the tax collector's prayer was real and from his heart. He was forgiven by God, but the Pharisee was not.

THINK: We must see that we are sinners and ask God to show mercy on us. The tax collector's prayer can be your prayer too, 'God be merciful to me a sinner.'

A rich young ruler came to Jesus one day. 'What must I do to have eternal life in heaven?' he asked.

'You know the commandments,' Jesus replied, 'Do not commit adultery. Do not kill. Do not steal. Do not tell lies. Honour your father and mother.'

'I have kept all these commandments since I was a boy,' he said.

But Jesus knew his weakness. 'Give all your money to the poor, then you will have treasure in heaven. Then follow me.'

The rich young man was very sad. He knew he could not do that. He loved his wealth too much.

'It is hard for a rich man to enter the kingdom of God,' Jesus told him. 'In fact it is easier for a camel to go through the eye of a needle!'

Those who were listening said, 'Who can be saved then?'

Jesus replied, 'What is impossible with men, is possible with God.'

THINK: We do not enter the Kingdom of God by our own efforts. Jesus has paid the price by dying on the cross for the sins of his people.

Jesus told this story. There was a rich man who dressed in beautiful clothes and lived in luxury. At the gate of his fine house lay a beggar called Lazarus. He was so hungry. He longed for a scrap of food from the rich man's table.

When Lazarus, the beggar, died he went to heaven with Abraham. The rich man died too but he went to the flames of hell. He was in agony. He called to Abraham, 'Send Lazarus to cool my tongue with a drop of water.'

'That is not possible,' replied Abraham. 'There is a great gulf fixed between heaven and hell. No one can cross over.'

'Send Lazarus to warn my brothers about this terrible place,' he asked Abraham.

'They can read the teachings of Moses and the prophets,' Abraham replied. 'If they do not listen to this teaching, they will not listen to anyone, not even someone who has risen from the dead.'

THINK: We have God's own Word, the Bible, which is sure and true and without error. God inspired different men to write his Word. It teaches what we are to believe about God and how we ought to behave.

Bartimaeus was blind. He could not work. He just sat by the roadside in Jericho begging. News was passed through the crowd that Jesus was coming along the road. Bartimaeus started to shout, 'Jesus, Son of David, have mercy on me!'

Some people told him to be quiet. But he shouted even more loudly, 'Have mercy on me.'

Jesus stopped and said, 'Call him over.' So they called Bartimaeus.

'Cheer up. Jesus is calling for you.'

Bartimaeus threw aside his cloak, jumped up and came to Jesus.

'What do you want me to do for you?' Jesus asked.

'I want to see,' he replied.

'Your faith has healed you,' Jesus told him.

Bartimaeus could see at once, and followed Jesus down the road.

THINK: We can pray that God would give us understanding to 'see' wonderful things in his Word.

253. Zacchaeus - Luke 19

Crowds of people lined the streets of Jericho to see Jesus. Zacchaeus, a tax collector, wanted to see him too but he was not tall enough to see over the crowd so he ran along the road and climbed a sycamore tree to get a good view.

When Jesus reached the spot, he looked up at him and said, 'Hurry down, Zacchaeus. I want to come to your house today.'

Zacchaeus was delighted to welcome Jesus to his home. The people grumbled. Zacchaeus was not popular. He was a rich man but had gained his wealth by cheating and charging too much tax money. When Zacchaeus met Jesus, he changed. 'I will give half of my wealth to the poor,' he told Jesus. 'If I cheated anyone, I will give back four times as much.'

Jesus said, 'Salvation has come to this house today. The Son of Man (Jesus himself) came to seek and to save the lost.'

THINK: Zacchaeus' life changed when he met Jesus. Jesus' saving power can cleanse the sinner from every sin.

One day Jesus was teaching in the temple courts and preaching the gospel. The teachers of the law and the chief priests were not pleased with Jesus' teaching. They wanted to catch him out, but Jesus dealt with them wisely, and the ordinary people listened.

Jesus noticed people putting money in the collection box. Rich people put in substantial amounts. A poor widow put in two very small copper coins.

Surprisingly Jesus said, 'This poor widow has put in more than all the others.' How could that be so?

Her small gift was all that she had to live on. Her giving was costly to her. The rich people had plenty. Their giving would not make any difference to their standard of living.

But these two small coins were a lot of money for the poor widow.

THINK: The Lord wants us to give him our lives and our love. He knows what is in our heart and mind.

Two men each built a house for himself and his family. Both wanted them to be safe and strong. One man built his house on rock which was a good firm foundation. He was wise. When the storm and rain came, the house was warm and safe.

Jesus said that if we hear what God tells us in the Bible and put it into practice in our lives, we are like the wise man. Our lives will be founded on a solid foundation and we will stand firm in the storms and difficulties of life.

If we hear God's Word and do not do what he tells us then we are like the foolish man.

He built his house on a foundation of sand. When the storms came, the foundation slipped, the bricks moved out of place and soon the house was in ruins.

If we do not obey God's Word, our lives will be in ruins too.

PRAY: Ask the Lord God that his Word would be the strong foundation of your life.

A wealthy man had to go on a long journey. He entrusted his servants with some of his property. To one he gave five talents of money, to another two and to a third one. A talent was a lot of money.

The first servant had made a good profit. When the master returned, he told him, 'I have increased your talent to ten.'

'Well done,' said the master. 'I will put you in charge of more.'

The second servant did well too. He doubled the money and was rewarded. The third servant stupidly dug a hole and buried the money. When the master returned, he dug it up and gave it back.

'You lazy servant! You have done nothing! I will take away what I gave you and give it to the first servant who has proved that he is faithful.'

THINK: Jesus wants us to understand that we should use what God has given us in his service.

Jesus told this story to teach us to keep on praying. We should never give up.

There was a judge in a town who only cared about himself. He did not bother about God or about other people.

A poor widow had a legal problem and needed the judge's help. She came to him day after day asking him to do justice for her. For a long time he refused her requests every day. Eventually he decided to do something to help the woman.

'I do not care what happens to this woman but she is becoming a nuisance. I had better do something before she wears me out completely.'

The unjust judge eventually listened to the persistent woman.

God is just and kind. He will listen to those people who persist in coming to him in prayer, asking for his help. Jesus wants us to keep on praying.

THINK: God is just and kind. He will listen to those people who persist in coming to him in prayer, asking for his help. Jesus wants us to keep on praying.

A landowner went out early one morning to hire workmen for his vineyard. He made a deal with the workers – the pay for working that day would be one silver coin.

Later that day, around nine, he noticed some men idle in the marketplace. 'Go and work in my vineyard,' he said. 'I will pay you a fair wage.'

At twelve o'clock and again at three, he did the same thing. Even at five o'clock he hired some men to work till darkness fell at six o'clock.

At six o'clock all the workers gathered to be paid. Each one was given one silver coin. The ones who had been there all day immediately complained.

'We have worked for longer than these others, why did we not get paid more?'

'I have not cheated you,' the owner replied. 'You agreed to do the day's work for one silver coin. Do not be jealous of my generosity to others.'

THINK: Heaven is the reward that Jesus prepares for all his people – the same for those who come to him late or early in life.

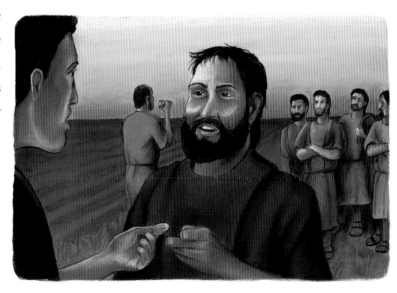

There was a landowner who planted a fine vineyard. He had to leave home for a long time, so he let out his vineyard to tenants. At harvest time he sent some of his servants to collect his share of the harvest. The tenants grabbed the servants, beat one, stoned another, even killed another.

The landowner sent other servants on the same errand but they were treated badly too.

'I will send my own dear son,' he said at last. 'Surely they will respect him.'

When the tenants saw the son, they plotted together. 'This is the owner's son,' they said. 'Come on, let's kill him. Then the vineyard will be ours.'

So they grabbed him, took him outside the vineyard and killed him.

Jesus told this story to teach a lesson. The landowner is like God. His servants are the prophets and teachers sent with God's Word to the world. Many were cruelly treated. God finally sent his only Son Jesus. He was cruelly treated and killed.

THINK: God wants us to know that his people are those who accept his Son as Lord and Saviour.

A man had two sons. One day the father said to the older boy, 'I need your help, son. Go and work in the vineyard for me.'

'No, I don't want to,' he answered. But later on he was sorry for what he had said, and went to work in the vineyard.

The father also went to the younger son and asked him to go and work in the vineyard.

'Yes, sir, of course,' he replied right away, sounding very willing to help. But he did not even turn up at the vineyard.

Which boy had done what his father wanted? The older one had done wrong at first, but he had repented.

Jesus taught in this story that our actions are more important than all the fine words we say.

THINK: Faith in Jesus Christ will lead to behaviour that is pleasing to God – loving him and obeying his Word and loving and caring for other people.

261. Forgiveness - Matthew 18

Once there was a king who decided to check his accounts to see if anyone owed him money.

One man was brought who owed him a huge sum of money. He had no money to pay the debt so the king ordered, 'Sell him as a slave with his wife and children. Sell all that he has.'

The man was very distressed. He fell on his knees and begged, 'Please be patient with me, I will pay you everything.' The king felt sorry for him, so he forgave the debt and let him go.

When the man went out, he met a friend who owed him a small amount. He roughly demanded payment. When the friend asked for forgiveness, he refused and had him thrown in jail.

When the king heard what happened, he was very angry. 'I forgave all that you owed. Should you not have done the same?'

God forgives his people when they repent and trust in the Lord Jesus. If we are forgiven so much, we should forgive others who do or say things against us.

PRAY: Thank God for the forgiveness he has shown you. Repent of your sin and turn to God.

Jesus wanted to explain how he cares for his people.

'I am the good shepherd,' he said. 'I know my sheep and my sheep know me.'

The sheep know the voice of the shepherd and follow him. Sheep will run away from strangers because they are afraid, but they trust the shepherd. The shepherd makes sure his sheep are safe.

Jesus, the good shepherd, loved his sheep so much that he gave his life for them.

A hired worker would get scared and run off when danger came, but because the sheep belong to the shepherd, he is prepared to give his life for them.

THINK: Jesus knows his people and loves them so much that he died for them on the cross at Calvary.

263. I am the Bread of Life - John 6

Jesus was able to satisfy over 5,000 hungry people with five loaves and two fishes.

He is also able to satisfy a much deeper hunger.

'I am the bread of life', Jesus said. 'He who comes to me will never be hungry. Whoever comes to me, I will never drive away.'

Some of the Jewish people grumbled when they heard the claims that Jesus made. They could not understand him. Did they not know his father and mother?

Jesus was not talking about ordinary bread. This bread from heaven satisfies the soul – giving assurance of God's love, peace and joy.

THINK: The one who eats this bread from heaven and trusts in Jesus alone, will never die but will have eternal life in heaven with God.

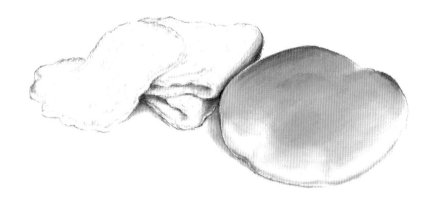

A vine is the tree that produces grapes. Jesus described himself as the true vine and his followers like the branches of that vine.

Unless the branch is attached to the vine it cannot bear fruit. Unless a person is connected to Jesus, his life will not be fruitful. Without Jesus Christ we can do nothing.

God, the Father, is like the gardener who looks for fruit on the branches. God expects the believer in Jesus to show fruit like love, joy and peace in his life.

If someone rejects the Lord Jesus Christ, it is as if the branch is cut from the tree and thrown into the fire.

PRAY: Ask God that your life would show fruit that proves that you are a disciple of Jesus. This gives glory to God, the Father.

Little children were brought by their parents to Jesus so that he would put his hands on them and pray for them.

The disciples were annoyed about this and tried to send them away. Perhaps they thought Jesus was too busy or that children were not important. Jesus thought differently.

'Let the little children come to me,' he said. 'Don't stop them. The kingdom of heaven belongs to them, and other children like them.'

Jesus placed his hands on them and blessed them.

When Jesus came to Jerusalem to face his death on the cross, he rode on a donkey. Crowds went ahead and behind, shouting, 'Hosanna in the highest!'

When he reached the temple, he healed many people. The children gathered round and shouted praise to Jesus. Jesus was pleased. He reminded the people that the book of Psalms tells that children and infants would praise the Lord.

THINK: No one is too young to need the Lord Jesus. No one is too young to trust in him.

Jesus and his disciples were walking towards the town of Nain. A large crowd of people joined them. As they approached the town gate, a funeral procession came out. A young man had died, the only son of his widowed mother.

When Jesus saw this poor widow who had just lost her only son, he felt very sorry for her. 'Don't cry,' he said.

Jesus went over and touched the coffin. Those carrying it stood still. 'Young man, get up!' said Jesus. The dead man sat up and began to talk. Jesus gave him back to his mother. What joy she must have felt.

The whole crowd of people was astonished and praised God. 'A great prophet has appeared amongst us,' they said. 'God has come to help his people.'

THINK: When we are sad, we can tell the Lord all about it. His Word will comfort us better than anything else.

Jesus was visiting Cana in Galilee. A royal official, whose son was very sick some miles away in Capernaum, begged for help.

Jesus challenged him, 'Unless you people see miraculous signs and wonders you will not believe.'

The royal official said to him, 'Sir, come down before my child dies.'

Jesus replied, 'You may go. Your son will live.'

The man believed Jesus and set off for home. When he was met by his servants, they told him his son was alive.

'When did he get better?' he asked them.

'The fever left him yesterday at the seventh hour,' they replied.

The father realised that this was the exact time Jesus had said, 'Your son will live.'

The royal official and all his family believed in Jesus.

THINK: Jesus performed this miracle to lead people to faith in him. When you read it you should also believe.

280

The pool of Bethesda in Jerusalem was surrounded by five covered porches. Many sick and disabled people gathered there, waiting for the waters to be disturbed by an angel, believing that the first person in would be healed. One man had been an invalid for thirty-eight years.

When Jesus saw him lying there, he said to him, 'Do you want to get well?'

'Sir,' he said. 'I have no one to help me into the pool. Someone always gets ahead of me.'

Jesus said, 'Get up! Pick up your mat and walk.' At once the man was cured. He picked up his mat and walked.

Some religious rulers objected that he was carrying his mat on the Sabbath day.

'The man who made me well told me to pick it up,' he replied.

He had no idea who had helped him for Jesus had slipped away into the crowd.

Later Jesus met him at the temple and warned him about his sin.

THINK: Sin is more damaging to our lives than any disease or disability. Jesus, the Saviour, is the only one who can deal with our sin.

Jesus met a man who had been born blind.

'Is this man blind because his parents sinned, or because he did something wrong?' the disciples asked.

'Neither he nor his parents are to blame,' Jesus replied. 'This has happened so that God's wonderful power can be shown in his life.'

Jesus spat on the ground, made some mud with the saliva and put it on the man's eyes.

'Go and wash in the pool of Siloam,' said Jesus. So the man went and washed his eyes. He went home, seeing for the first time.

His neighbours could hardly believe it. 'That must be another man that looks like our neighbour,' some insisted.

'No, I am the man.'

When they asked what had happened, the man explained all that Jesus had done and said.

THINK: As a result of Jesus' power, the man could see, but, more importantly, he believed in Jesus.

A foreign woman from the area around Tyre came to Jesus begging for help. 'Lord,' she cried, 'have mercy on me. My daughter is tormented by evil spirits.'

At first Jesus did not answer. 'Send her away,' the disciples urged him. 'She keeps annoying us.'

Jesus spoke to her, 'I was sent to serve the people of Israel.'

The woman came and knelt before him, 'Lord, help me,' she prayed.

'If I help you, a foreigner,' said Jesus. 'It would be like taking the children's bread and tossing it to a dog.'

'Yes, Lord,' the woman said boldly, 'but even the dogs eat the crumbs that fall from the master's table.'

'You have great faith,' Jesus responded. 'I will do as you ask.'

At that very moment her daughter was healed.

PRAY: God's family is made up of people from every nation. Pray today for Christians in a foreign land.

Jesus and his disciples made their way to Capernaum. In the house, Jesus asked them, 'What were you arguing about on the road?' Nobody wanted to answer the question, because they had been arguing about which of them was the greatest.

Jesus knew their thoughts. He sat down and started to explain how God's view of greatness was not the same as theirs. To help them understand he called a little boy over to stand beside him.

'Unless you become like a little child you will never enter the kingdom of heaven,' he said. 'The greatest in the kingdom of heaven is the one who is as humble as this little child.'

'The person who welcomes a little child like this one is welcoming me,' added Jesus. 'The person who welcomes me is also welcoming God who sent me.'

THINK: Jesus wants children to trust in him and believe his Word.

Jesus told this story about a girl who had ten bridesmaids. Five of them were wise. They had brought plenty of oil to keep their lamps burning all night, as they waited to escort the bridegroom to the wedding. Five of them were foolish. They did not take any extra oil.

The bridegroom was a long time in coming, so they all dropped off to sleep. At midnight, someone shouted, 'The bridegroom is on his way. Get ready to meet him.'

'Our lamps are beginning to go out,' wailed the five foolish girls. 'Give us some of yours.'

'Not at all,' replied the wise girls. 'Go and buy some for yourselves.'

When they were away the bridegroom arrived. The five wise girls greeted him and went into the wedding feast. The door was shut. The foolish girls tried to get in when they came back but they were too late.

THINK: We need to be ready to meet the Lord Jesus when we die or when he comes again. The only way to be ready is to repent of our sins and to have faith in Christ Jesus.

285

Some Greek people came to Jerusalem to worship at the feast. They came up to Philip and asked, 'Sir, we would like to see Jesus.' Philip went to tell Andrew and then they both went to tell Jesus.

Jesus told them that the hour had come for him to be glorified. A wheat seed only produces more seeds if it is put into the ground and dies. Jesus was warning them that he was about to die.

'My heart is troubled', he said. 'Shall I ask my Father to save me from this hour? No, it was for this very reason that I came. Father glorify your name.'

A voice came from heaven, 'I have glorified it and I will glorify it again.' The crowd heard God's voice and thought it was thunder, or that an angel had spoken.

'When I am lifted up from the earth', Jesus said, 'I will draw all men to myself.' This was indicating that he would die lifted up on a cross and Jew and Gentile would be saved by him.

PRAY: Thank God for loving the world so much that he sent his Son so that those who believe in him, would be saved from eternal punishment in hell.

On the road to Jerusalem, Jesus stopped at the Mount of Olives overlooking the city.

'Go to that village over there,' he told two of his disciples. 'You will find a young donkey. Bring it to me. If anyone asks you what you are doing, tell them the Lord needs this donkey.'

The disciples brought the young donkey and put some of their clothes on its back.

Jesus rode into Jerusalem. Crowds of people joined the procession.

Some cut down branches from the palm trees and placed them on the ground in front of Jesus. Others laid down their cloaks.

The crowd shouted out joyfully, 'Hosanna to the Son of David! Blessed is he that comes in the name of the Lord!'

Jesus rode right into the town.

THINK: The word 'hosanna' means 'please save'. We can praise God, the Son, by asking him to save us from sin.

287

When Jesus arrived in Jerusalem he went to the temple. In the courtyard he saw greedy men using the temple as a trading place. They were selling doves and exchanging money. Honest people were being cheated.

'My house is called a house of prayer,' Jesus said, 'but you have made it a den of robbers.'

Jesus overturned the tables of the money-changers and the benches of those selling the doves. He would not allow anyone to carry goods for sale into the temple courtyard.

Blind and lame people came to the temple to see Jesus and he healed them. The children sang praises to Jesus.

All this made the chief priests and lawyers very annoyed.

THINK. Children realised that Jesus was truly God and ought to be worshipped. You are not too young to worship Jesus.

The Pharisees were enemies of Jesus and hated his teachings.

One day they tried to trap Jesus into saying something wrong. They sent some men to him with flattering words to ask him a trick question.

'Teacher,' they said, 'we know you are a man of integrity and teach the way of God. You are not swayed by public opinion. Tell us then, is it right to pay taxes to Caesar or not?'

Jesus knew they were trying to trap him.

'Show me a penny,' he told them.

They brought to him the coin used for paying tax.

'Whose portrait and inscription is on it?' Jesus asked.

'Caesar's,' they replied.

'Give to Caesar, what is Caesar's,' Jesus told them, 'and to God what is God's.'

They were all amazed at Jesus' wise answer. He had not fallen into their trap.

They all left him alone.

THINK: It is right to respect the laws of our land, but even more important to honour God and his holy Word.

Jesus sent two of his disciples to prepare the Passover Feast in Jerusalem.

'You will meet a man carrying a jar of water,' Jesus said. Carrying water was usually a woman's work, so it would have been easy to spot a man doing that. 'This man will lead you to a house,' Jesus added. 'Explain to the owner that we will need a room where we can eat the Passover Feast. He will show you to a large upstairs room. Get everything ready there.'

They followed the instructions and in the evening Jesus arrived with the rest of the disciples.

This was a very special Passover Feast. Jesus was preparing himself and his disciples for his death. This was the last supper they ate together.

THINK: The Passover Feast was held every year to remind the people of God's delivering them from slavery to Pharaoh in Egypt. The next story shows you what Christians do today to remember Jesus death.

Jesus and his disciples all sat down around the table.

Jesus broke the bread, after giving thanks for it and handed it round. 'This is my body,' he said, 'broken for you. Do this in remembrance of me.'

Then he passed round a cup of wine. 'This is my blood,' he said. 'When you eat the bread and drink the wine, remember me.'

Jesus knew the suffering that was to come to him. He went willingly to the cross to pay the price for the sin of his followers, those who love him and trust him.

Followers of Jesus still remember his death when they take the Lord's Supper as Communion. The broken bread is a symbol of Jesus' body as he suffered pain and agony on the cross.

THINK: This feast is to remind us of God delivering his people from slavery to sin.

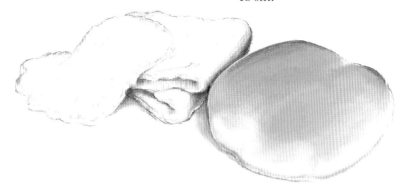

279. Jesus Washes his Disciples' Feet - John 13

As the meal was being served, Jesus got up from the table. He took off his coat and wrapped a towel around his waist.

He poured water into a basin and began to wash his disciples' feet, and dried them with his towel.

The disciples were surprised that their Master would perform such a lowly task for them.

When he had finished, Jesus put his coat back on and returned to his place at the table.

'I am your Lord and Master,' he said, 'and you have just seen me wash your feet. Now you should follow my example.'

Jesus was teaching his disciples and us not to be proud and feel important but to serve each other humbly and care for one another.

PRAY: Ask God the Father to help you to be humble and to be willing to care for others.

Jesus spoke with his disciples for many hours, warning them of the difficult days ahead.

'I am giving you a new commandment,' Jesus said, 'You must love one another. Everyone will know you are my disciples if you love one another.'

'You will all be ashamed of me tonight,' Jesus told them.

Peter answered boldly, 'I will never be ashamed of you, even if everyone else is.'

'I am telling you, Peter,' Jesus replied, 'before the cock crows in the morning, you will deny three times that you even know me.'

'I would never deny you,' exclaimed Peter, 'even if I had to die with you!'

Peter sounded very brave but Jesus was right.

PRAY: Ask God that he would teach you not to be boastful, and to realise how much we need his help every day.

We learn about Jesus by overhearing one of his prayers.

He would give eternal life to all those whom his Father had given him. This eternal life he described as knowing God and Jesus Christ whom God had sent.

He prayed for his people down through the ages, not just his disciples living then, but all his followers right to our day. Jesus still prays for his people – those who trust in him.

Jesus glorified his Father by being obedient and doing the work in this world that he was given to do. God the Father would honour him.

Jesus keeps and guards his followers and reveals God to them through his Word.

Jesus prayed that his followers would be united just as he and his Father were united, so that the world would know that God had sent his Son.

THINK: Be thankful that Jesus, the Son of God, is praying in heaven for his people all the time.

Jesus and his disciples went to a garden called Gethsemane.

'Sit here,' he said, 'while I go over there to pray.'

He took Peter and James and John with him. 'I am troubled,' he said. 'Stay here and keep me company.'

He went a little further and fell down on his face and prayed to God his Father. He was in agony thinking about the suffering that was just ahead of him. God sent an angel from heaven to strengthen Jesus.

When he came back to the disciples, they were sleeping. 'Could you not keep awake for even one hour?' Jesus asked Peter.

Jesus went to pray again. Again the disciples could not keep awake. They did not know what to say to Jesus.

'Wake up!' said Jesus. 'You must pray that God will keep you from temptation.'

PRAY: Ask the Lord that he would keep you from sin and help you to fight against temptation.

283. Jesus is Arrested - Matthew 26, John 18

A group of people approached Jesus. Among them was Judas Iscariot. He had made an arrangement with Jesus' enemies. They gave Judas thirty silver coins. 'I will point out Jesus to you by giving him a kiss,' Judas agreed.

Jesus knew what was to happen. He bravely approached the crowd.

'Who are you looking for?' he asked.

'Jesus of Nazareth,' they replied.

'I am he,' Jesus said simply.

Judas and the men were startled by Jesus' straight reply. Judas carried out the arranged plan. 'Master,' he greeted Jesus, giving him a kiss.

When the disciples saw what was happening, they wanted to fight. Peter lashed out with a sword and cut off the ear of the high priest's servant.

'No more of this!' said Jesus. He touched the man's ear and it was immediately healed.

The soldiers caught hold of Jesus, tied him up and led him to the high priest's palace.

THINK: The Lord Jesus was gracious even when he was being arrested. He took time to heal the man's ear.

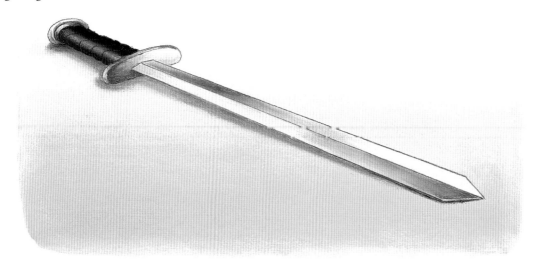

Peter and another disciple followed Jesus to the high priest's palace. A young girl who worked there recognised Peter. 'This man was with Jesus too,' she said.

'I don't know him,' snapped Peter.

He moved out to the porch as the cock first crowed. Someone else saw Peter in the porch. 'Aren't you one of them too?' he asked.

'I am not!' said Peter.

An hour later a man said to Peter, 'Surely you are one of Jesus' followers, for you speak like them.'

Peter replied roughly, 'I don't know what you are talking about. I do not know the man!'

Immediately the cock crowed for the second time. Jesus turned round and looked at Peter. Peter remembered what Jesus had said, 'Before the cock crows twice, you will deny me three times.' Peter went out and wept bitterly. He had failed the Lord Jesus.

THINK: Jesus knew all about Peter. He had warned Peter that he would deny him. He knows all about us too.

Jesus was taken before Pilate, the Roman Governor. 'What is this man accused of?' Pilate asked.

'This man says things against our nation. He says he is Christ, a king.'

'Are you really the King of the Jews?' asked Pilate.

'My kingdom is not worldly,' Jesus replied. 'The whole purpose of my life in this world is to tell people the truth.'

'I do not find him guilty of any crime,' said Pilate.

The crowd would not accept that so Pilate passed him on to Herod, the king. Herod and the soldiers mocked Jesus and sent him back to Pilate.

'Perhaps I could release Jesus,' suggested Pilate. 'I am allowed to release a prisoner at Passover time.'

'No,' shouted the crowd. 'Crucify him. Crucify him!'

Pilate tried to reason with the crowd but they were insistent that Jesus would be put to death on a cross. 'Crucify him!' they chanted.

Eventually Pilate gave in to their demands. He listened to the rabble rather than his own conscience.

PRAY: Ask God to help you to do the right thing, even when other people are insisting that you do something wrong.

Jesus was led away to a place, outside the city wall, called Calvary. This was a terrible place where common criminals were executed by crucifixion. Jesus was whipped and beaten and mocked by the soldiers. They forced him to wear a crown of thorns. He was already tired and bleeding before he reached Calvary. He had to carry a large wooden cross.

Jesus was nailed to this cross by his hands and feet and left to hang there in terrible pain until he died several hours later.

His suffering and death were fulfilling a wonderful plan of salvation for his people. All sin deserves to be punished. By suffering and dying for the sin of his own people who trust in him, Jesus took the full punishment for all their sins.

What love he showed. Even when the men were nailing him to the cross, Jesus prayed to God, 'Father, forgive them for they do not know what they are doing.'

PRAY: Thank God for sending his Son to this earth, to die in the place of sinners like you. He is the Lamb of God, the perfect sacrifice for sin.

The soldiers took Jesus' garment and cut it into four parts. Each of them took a piece. His coat was made of one piece of material with no seams. 'Let's not tear it up,' one of them said. 'Let's cast lots and the winner can take it all.'

Even that small detail had been foretold in the book of Psalms many years before.

Jesus' mother, Mary, and some other women were standing near the cross, watching what was happening to Jesus. Mary must have been heartbroken. Even during his pain, Jesus noticed his mother and his disciple, John.

Jesus said to his mother, 'Look on John as your son now.'

To John he said, 'Treat Mary like your mother.'

From then on John took Mary into his own home to look after her.

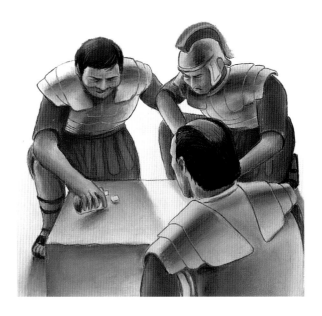

THINK: All the details of your life are well known to God. He has a plan for your life too.

Two other men were crucified at the same time as Jesus, one on either side of him. Both were thieves.

One of the thieves complained to Jesus, 'If you really are Christ, why can't you save yourself and us?'

The other one was indignant.

'How can you speak like that?' he said. 'We deserve all this punishment, but this man has done nothing wrong.'

Then he turned to Jesus and said, 'Remember me when you come into your kingdom.'

'Today you shall be with me in heaven,' Jesus assured him.

This man believed in Jesus even at the end of his life and received God's salvation.

PRAY: Thank God for his loving mercy which reached out to this thief even after such a sinful life.

After being on the cross for six hours, Jesus reached the depths of his suffering. He called out to God, 'My God, my God, why have you left me?' Jesus was so alone, bearing the punishment for the sins of his people whose place he was taking.

When he called out, 'I am thirsty!' he was given a sponge soaked in vinegar.

After Jesus had drunk some vinegar, he called out, 'It is finished!' and then with a loud voice, 'Father, into your hands I commend my spirit.'

He then bowed his head and died.

At that moment the curtain in the temple was torn in two from top to bottom, the earth trembled, the rocks split open and even some graves opened.

When one soldier saw all this happening, he was very afraid. 'Certainly this was the Son of God,' he confessed.

THINK: Jesus suffered so much. He was even left by his Father, completely forsaken, so that we are never left by God. 'I will never leave you or forsake you,' he promised.

A rich man called Joseph, who was a secret follower of Jesus, went boldly to Pilate and asked if he might have Jesus' body to bury him in his own tomb. His request was granted so Joseph, helped by Nicodemus, took Jesus' body and wrapped it in a linen cloth. They carried the body through a garden and laid it carefully in the tomb which was a cave. They rolled a big stone over the mouth of the cave.

The chief priests and religious leaders remembered that Jesus had said he would rise from the dead on the third day. 'Give orders that the tomb is made very secure until the third day,' they said to Pilate, 'just in case his disciples come and steal his body and say he is risen.'

'Go,' said Pilate, 'and make it as secure as you can.'

So the stone was specially sealed in front of the guard.

THINK: God gave Joseph and Nicodemus the courage to confess their love for the Lord Jesus openly. Ask God to give you the courage to stand up for Jesus too.

Very early in the morning on the first day of the week, Mary Magdalene and two other ladies came to the tomb. They wanted to anoint Jesus' body with spices. They discussed a problem on the way. 'How are we going to get the stone rolled away from the entrance to the tomb?'

When they reached the tomb, what a surprise they got. The stone had been rolled away already.

Mary Magdalene rushed to find Peter and John. 'Someone has taken away the Lord's body and I do not know where they have put him,' she said.

Meantime, the other ladies crept right into the tomb. There they saw two men in dazzling white clothes – angels of the Lord. The women were frightened.

'Do not be afraid,' said one angel. 'I know you are looking for Jesus, who was crucified. He is not here. He has risen from the dead on the third day. Go and tell his disciples, especially Peter, that he has risen from the dead.'

THINK: God raised Jesus from the dead (called the Resurrection) proving that he accepted his sacrifice for the sin of his people. This gives us the hope of salvation and great joy.

Peter and John came running when they heard the news from Mary Magdalene. They looked into the tomb and saw the linen grave clothes lying where Jesus had been. Peter and John went back home wondering at all the things that had happened.

Mary Magdalene came back to the garden. She was weeping with sorrow because she thought that Jesus' body had been stolen. A man came to speak to her.

'Why are you crying?' he asked. 'Who are you looking for?'

She thought this man was the gardener. 'Sir,' she said, 'if you have taken him away, please tell me where you have laid his body.'

The man said to her, 'Mary!'

She then realised that the man was the risen Lord Jesus.

'Master!' she cried out.

Mary and her two friends brought word to the rest of the disciples.

THINK: When we have good news we should pass it on to others. The best news is the gospel, telling us about salvation from sin by the Lord Jesus Christ.

The disciples met together in a room with the doors tightly shut. They were afraid that the people would kill them too.

Just then a really wonderful thing happened. Jesus came into the room although the doors were shut.

He spoke to them, 'Peace be to you,' he said.

Jesus showed them his hands which had been pierced by the nails on the cross, and his side which had been pierced by a spear.

The disciples were overjoyed to see Jesus again. 'I am sending you out to the world, just as God sent me,' he told them.

He breathed on them, 'Receive the Holy Spirit. Now you have power to do God's work, just as I have.'

THINK: The disciples were so glad when they met Jesus. We should be glad when we meet with Jesus in his Word, the Bible.

Thomas was not with the other disciples when Jesus first appeared to them. When the other disciples told him what had happened, he refused to believe. 'Unless I see the marks of the nails in his hands and put my hand into the wound in his side, I will not believe.'

A week later the disciples were in the same house but this time Thomas was there too. Though the doors were locked, Jesus came and stood among them. He turned to Thomas. 'Put your finger here in my hands. Put your hand into my side. Stop doubting and believe.'

'My Lord and my God,' Thomas confessed.

'You believe me because you have seen me,' Jesus said. 'Blessed are those people who have not seen me, yet still believe.'

THINK: Think about some of the blessings that Jesus gives to those who believe in him – forgiveness of sin, peace, joy and much more.

295. Road to Emmaus - Luke 24

Cleopas and a friend were walking from Jerusalem to Emmaus, about seven miles away. They were discussing the amazing events of the past few days in Jerusalem.

Jesus himself came and walked beside them but they did not recognise him.

'What have you been speaking about?' he asked.

'Don't you know what has been happening in Jerusalem?' they exclaimed.

'What things?' Jesus replied.

'The things that happened to Jesus,' they answered. Jesus gently rebuked the men. 'You are so slow to believe what has been told you by the prophets. Christ had to suffer all these things before he entered his glory.'

Jesus then explained to them all the Old Testament Scriptures which referred to himself.

THINK: Jesus is with us always, even when we are not aware of it. There is not a moment of any day or night when God is not looking after us. He never slumbers or sleeps.

When they came to Emmaus, Jesus seemed to intend carrying on further.

They begged him, 'Please stay with us. It is late now.'

Jesus went into the house with them and sat down for supper. He took the bread, blessed it and broke off a piece for each of them.

Only then did they recognise the risen Lord Jesus. Immediately, he vanished from their sight.

'That explains how we felt as he spoke to us on the road, explaining the Scriptures to us,' they said to each other.

With no delay they walked back to Jerusalem to share their wonderful news with the eleven disciples.

'The Lord is risen indeed!'

THINK: When we realise who Jesus is, we should be enthusiastic to tell others.

One evening some time later, several disciples were together by the Sea of Galilee.

'I am going to go fishing,' said Peter.

'We will go too,' said the others.

They fished all night but caught nothing. When the morning came they saw a man on the shore watching them. 'Have you anything to eat?' he called out.

'No,' they replied.

'Put your net out on the right side of the boat,' he told them, 'then you will find fish.'

When they did this, the net became so full of fish that they could not pull it into the boat. John then realised that the man on the shore was Jesus. 'It is the Lord,' he gasped.

Peter pulled on his coat and dived into the water to swim to the shore as fast as he could. The others followed in the boat, dragging the net full of fish behind them. They ate a meal of fish and bread on the shore.

THINK: Remember that there is a blessing for us in obeying what Jesus tells us to do.

After breakfast on the shore, Jesus turned to Peter and, using his other name, asked, 'Simon, do you love me?'

'Yes Lord, you know that I love you,' Peter answered.

'Feed my lambs,' Jesus told him.

Again Jesus said, 'Simon, do you love me?'

'Yes, Lord, you know that I love you,' Peter answered again.

'Feed my sheep,' said Jesus.

Jesus asked the same question a third time, 'Simon, do you love me?'

Peter was upset at being asked a third time and he said to Jesus, 'Lord, you know everything. You know that I love you.'

'Feed my sheep,' Jesus told him again.

Peter had now said three times that he loved Jesus. Perhaps he remembered with shame that he had denied Jesus three times.

Jesus had forgiven him. He wanted Peter to feed his lambs and sheep – that means to spread the gospel to people old and young.

THINK: Even if we go astray like Peter, Jesus will welcome us back when we come to him. Jesus still wants to use us to spread the gospel.

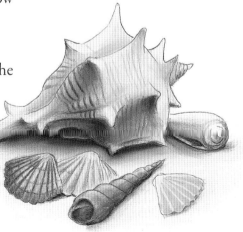

299. Go Into All the World - Matthew 28

In the forty days after Jesus rose from the dead he appeared many times. Many people met him. He appeared to Mary Magdalene, other women, Peter, ten disciples, then eleven disciples including Thomas, two people on the road to Emmaus, 500 people at once and to James and the apostles. There could be no doubt that Jesus was alive.

One day Jesus met with the eleven disciples on a hill above the Sea of Galilee. 'I have been given all authority over heaven and earth. Now you must go and make disciples of all nations. Baptise the disciples in the name of God the Father, God the Son and God the Holy Spirit. Teach them to obey everything I have commanded you. I will be with you always.'

Jesus' disciples are all over the world today. Jesus is with each one of them by His Spirit.

PRAY: Thank God for the truth of the resurrection. Jesus really is alive. That is wonderful.

Jesus and his disciples went out to the Mount of Olives and Bethany.

Jesus spoke to them about the future. 'I will send the Holy Spirit to help you. You will be my witnesses in Jerusalem and Judea and Samaria, right to the furthest corners of the earth.'

As he said these words he lifted up his hands and blessed them. He was lifted into heaven, right through the clouds. The disciples were astounded. They stood gazing up into the sky where Jesus had gone.

Two men in white clothes stood beside them.

'Why are you standing there staring? Just as you have seen Jesus being taken up into heaven, he will return to earth one day.'

This filled the disciples with joy. They worshipped God and went back to Jerusalem to start preaching the good news of the Word of God.

THINK: We are made to worship God and to enjoy him forever.

5. The Apostles and the Early Church

Books of the Bible:

Acts of The Apostles

What you will read about:

Peter, John, Philip, Paul, Silas, Barnabas,
Lydia, Timothy, Priscilla and Aquila,
Paul's Journeys and his Arrest

Before he ascended into heaven, Jesus told the disciples to return to Jerusalem and wait there for the Holy Spirit to be sent to help them witness for him.

So the eleven disciples – Peter, John, James, Andrew, Philip, Thomas, Bartholomew, Matthew, another James, Simon, and Judas – gathered in an upstairs room with Mary, Jesus' mother, some other women and Jesus' brothers. They spent all the time praying.

Judas Isacariot, who had betrayed Jesus, was not there. He had been so filled with remorse after Jesus' death, that he killed himself.

'We must choose another disciple to replace Judas Iscariot,' Peter said. 'This will fulfil what was written long ago in the book of Psalms. We should pick someone who knew Jesus well and who was a witness to the resurrection.'

Two names were put forward – Joseph and Matthias. After prayers for guidance, Matthias was picked to be one of the apostles.

THINK: Remember that the Holy Spirit is God. He is a helper and teacher to God's people.

People from many nations were visiting Jerusalem for the feast of Pentecost. This feast was on the fiftieth day after the Passover Feast.

The disciples, now called apostles, were together in one house. Suddenly the noise of a strong wind filled the house. Separate tongues of fire rested on each one of them.

God, the Holy Spirit filled them with his power, as Jesus had promised. This meant that they could speak God's Word to the crowds in Jerusalem, and each man heard what the apostles were saying in his own language.

Many were astonished by the power of God, but others laughed at the apostles. 'They have had too much wine,' they jeered.

Peter stood up and addressed the crowd. 'We have not drunk any wine,' he said, 'it is only nine o'clock in the morning.' Peter then began to preach God's Word and the good news of Jesus Christ to the people.

THINK: All Jesus' promises are true. The Holy Spirit gave power just as Jesus had promised.

Peter started to preach powerfully to the crowd. 'Listen to this. Let me tell you about Jesus.' Peter reminded them of the miracles and wonderful things Jesus had done. He told them how Jesus had been put to death on the cross by wicked men but this was all in God's plan. God raised him from the dead. Jesus is Lord and Christ.

The people were cut to the heart by Peter's preaching.

'What shall we do?' they said.

Peter urged them to repent – turn from sin – to accept Jesus' forgiveness of sin and to be baptised in the name of Jesus Christ.

On that one day about 3,000 people believed in Jesus Christ and put their trust in Him.

THINK: We need to be truly sorry for our sins (or repent) and ask Jesus to forgive us.

These people who trusted in Jesus loved listening to the apostles teaching about the Word of God. They learned more and more about Jesus. They met together to pray. They spoke together and had meals together. They shared their possessions. They sold what they did not need to help another believer who did need something.

They praised God and showed great kindness to others.

Day by day more and more people heard the good news of the gospel and put their trust in the Lord Jesus, to save them from their sins.

The people who believe in the Lord Jesus Christ are known as 'the church.'

PRAY: Thank God for your church family who meet together for prayer, worship and teaching about the Word of God.

305. A Lame Beggar is Healed - Acts 3

One afternoon Peter and John went to the temple to pray. At the Beautiful Gate a lame man sat begging. He asked Peter and John for money.

'I have no silver or gold,' Peter told him, 'but I will give you something else. In the name of Jesus Christ get up and walk.'

He took him by the right hand and pulled him to his feet. Immediately, he felt strength surging into his feet and ankles. He was able to walk for the first time ever. He went into the temple with Peter and John jumping for joy and praising God.

The people recognised him and could hardly believe that he was the same man who used to sit begging at the gate.

THINK: God loves to hear praise. Praise him and thank him for all his goodness to you.

The priests and temple rulers were really disturbed because the apostles were teaching the people about Jesus and his resurrection. Many people believed the gospel and the number of believers grew to 5,000. The rulers seized Peter and John and because it was late in the day, put them in prison overnight.

The next day Peter and John were brought before the rulers.

'How did you heal the lame man at the temple gate?' they asked.

Peter was helped to reply by God the Holy Spirit.

'The lame man was healed by the power of Jesus Christ of Nazareth whom you crucified but whom God raised from the dead. Salvation is found in no one else. There is no other name under heaven given to men by which we must be saved.'

THINK: Remember there is no other way to be saved from sin apart from trusting in the Lord Jesus Christ who died for sinners.

The religious leaders were astonished to hear ordinary, uneducated men like Peter speak so courageously. They knew that they had been with Jesus. They did not know what to do. Peter and John were sent out and the leaders conferred together.

'What are we going to do with these men?' they asked. 'We cannot deny a miracle has happened. But we must stop them speaking to others.'

They called Peter and John back in and forbade them to speak or teach in the name of Jesus.

'Do you think it is right to obey you rather than God?' Peter and John replied. 'We cannot help speaking about what we have seen and heard.'

After some threatening remarks, they let Peter and John go.

THINK: If you know and love Jesus, people should see this from what you do and say.

One couple called Ananias and Sapphira decided to sell their land. Ananias took the money to Peter.

'Here's all the money we got for our land,' he said. But he was lying. They had kept some of the money for themselves. Peter knew he was not telling the truth. He said to Ananias, 'The land was yours. The money was yours. Why did you pretend to give all the money? You have lied to God.'

When Ananias heard these words, he fell down dead.

Three hours later Sapphira returned, not knowing what happened to her husband.

'Did you really sell the land for so much?' Peter asked.

'Oh yes,' she lied.

'Oh, you have agreed together to cheat God, the Holy Spirit. The men who have buried your husband are at the door. They will carry your body out to be buried too,' said Peter. Immediately she dropped down dead.

THINK: God hates lying. He wants us to tell the truth. Ask God to help you to tell the truth and to forgive you when you are untruthful.

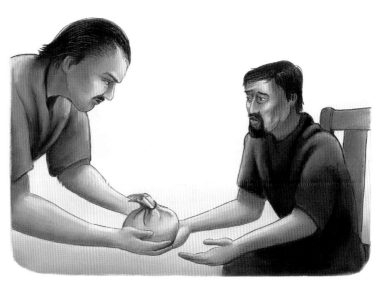

Stephen was a devout follower of the Lord Jesus. He did many miracles through God's power. He spoke wisely by the help of the Holy Spirit.

Some lawyers wickedly persuaded men to accuse Stephen falsely with blasphemy against God. He was brought before the high court. As he stood up to reply to his accusers, his face shone like an angel. The Lord was with him, helping him to find the right words.

Stephen looked up to heaven and said, 'I see heaven open and Jesus standing at the right hand of God.'

The Jewish priests became enraged with all Stephen had said. They dragged him out of the city. They picked up big stones and hurled them at Stephen.

'Lord Jesus, receive my spirit,' he prayed.

Just before he died, he prayed for the people who were killing him. 'Lord, do not hold this sin against them.'

Stephen showed real love to his enemies.

THINK: Jesus taught us to love our enemies. He prayed for them when he was dying too.

Philip, a deacon from Jerusalem, preached about Jesus Christ in Samaria. Many people flocked to hear him. An angel spoke to Philip telling him to go on a journey. He started out south on the desert road to Gaza. Soon he met an Ethiopian man, an official of the queen of Ethiopia. He was reading a scroll from the writings of Isaiah in his chariot.

God guided Philip to approach the chariot.

'Do you understand what you are reading?' Philip asked.

'How can I?' he replied, 'unless someone explains it to me. Come up here and sit with me.'

He was reading about the lamb led to the slaughter in Isaiah 53. Philip explained that Isaiah was speaking about the Lord Jesus. He went on to tell about the good news of Jesus as they drove along the road.

'Why shouldn't I be baptised in the water over there?' the Ethiopian asked.

So Philip baptised the Ethiopian. He now believed in the Lord Jesus.

PRAY: Thank God for someone who has explained the Bible to you. The best teacher of all is the Holy Spirit.

Saul was born in Tarsus in a country we now call Turkey. His parents were Jewish. Saul grew up learning the law of God in great detail. As a young man he went to Jerusalem to study under a famous teacher, Gamaliel. He was studious and law-abiding. He became a teacher of the Jewish law, and learned how to make tents.

Saul was a strict religious law-keeper. He hated the followers of Jesus who were growing in number. Saul did all he could to hurt those who believed that Jesus Christ had died for their sins.

Saul was present when many people were throwing stones at Stephen because he told them about Jesus. Saul looked on in approval and even took care of the coats the men had taken off.

Saul hated Jesus and all the people that followed him. He was sent to Damascus with official letters. His plan was to find any follower of Jesus, arrest them, then take them back to Jerusalem to be punished.

PRAY: Jesus' love reaches to the very worst of sinners. His power can change the hardest heart.

Around midday Saul came near to Damascus. Suddenly a bright light shone from heaven. Saul threw himself on the ground, terrified. He heard a voice saying, 'Saul, Saul, why are you persecuting me?'

'Who are you, Lord?' Saul answered.

The voice replied, 'I am Jesus of Nazareth, whom you are persecuting. Get up and go into the city and you will be told what to do.'

The people with Saul saw the light and were very afraid. Saul was trembling with fear too.

Saul rose from the ground. When he opened his eyes, he found that he could not see. The dazzling bright light had blinded him.

He was led by the hand on the rest of the journey to Damascus and taken to the house of Judas in Straight Street.

For three days he was blind and did not eat or drink anything.

THINK: Jesus is still meeting with sinners. In his Word he confronts us with our sins and tells us that we can receive mercy and forgiveness.

Saul spent three days praying to God. God heard his prayer and sent someone to help him.

Ananias, a follower of the Lord Jesus, lived in Damascus. God spoke to him in a vision.

'Go to Straight Street, to Judas' house and ask for a man called Saul from Tarsus. He is praying there.'

Ananias was nervous. 'I have heard about that man, Lord,' he said. 'He has done a lot of harm to your people in Jerusalem. He has permission to come here to arrest those who follow you.'

'Go!' the Lord reassured him, 'for I have chosen him to preach about me to all sorts of people.'

Ananias found Saul where God had told him.

'Brother Saul,' he said, 'the Lord Jesus who spoke to you on the road here, has sent me to you so that you may receive your sight back. You will be filled with the Holy Spirit too.'

Immediately something like scales fell from Saul's eyes and he could see again.

THINK: Saul's life was completely turned around by the Lord Jesus. He was converted through repentance and faith in Jesus Christ.

Saul was baptised to show that he was now a believer in the Lord Jesus Christ. He had begun a new life. He then ate a good meal which gave him strength.

The believers in Damascus welcomed Saul. He preached about Jesus in the synagogue, passing on the good news that Jesus is the Son of God.

Saul preached so powerfully in Damascus, that the Jews were very upset. Eventually they plotted to kill Saul. Saul heard about this wicked plot. He would have to escape. The Jews set guards on watch at all the gates of the city, to make sure they would catch him.

The believers (now Saul's friends) made a good plan. They got hold of a large basket. Saul slipped inside it and his friends carefully let the basket down by ropes over the city wall. In this way Saul escaped.

PRAY: Thank God for your friends and those who help you in difficult times. They are a blessing from God.

315. Saul Changed - Acts 9

In Jerusalem the followers of Jesus were afraid when Saul tried to join them. They remembered how cruel he had been when he was in Jerusalem before. They could hardly believe that he was a different man.

A kind man called Barnabas spoke up for Saul.

'He really has changed. The Lord Jesus met him on the road to Damascus. He has already preached boldly in Damascus about the Lord.'

Saul was accepted as their friend and brother. He went around Jerusalem, speaking boldly in the name of the Lord. The dramatic change in Saul's life was caused by his meeting with the Lord Jesus. Saul later wrote, 'Jesus Christ came into the world to save sinners. I am the worst sinner but I was shown mercy.'

THINK: Jesus still shows mercy to sinners. The Bible tells us that we too can receive the same mercy and forgiveness that Saul did by trusting in Jesus alone.

Peter travelled round the country telling people the good news of the gospel. One day he came to visit the believers in Lydda. There he met a man who had been in bed for eight years, unable to walk.

'Aeneas,' Peter said to him, 'Jesus Christ makes you whole, get up and tidy up your bed.'

Aeneas immediately got up.

Many people who saw this wonderful happening came to believe in the Lord.

The town of Joppa was nearby. Some believers lived there too, among them a lady called Dorcas.

The news of Aeneas' recovery reached the people in Joppa.

THINK: The good news of the gospel has travelled from person to person and place to place. Thank God that the gospel message has reached you.

Dorcas spent her time helping others. She made coats and dresses for the local poor children and their mothers.

One day Dorcas fell ill and died. Her friends were very upset. What would they do without Dorcas to help them?

'Someone should go to Lydda and fetch Peter,' someone suggested. 'He may be able to help.'

As soon as Peter was asked he went with the men to Dorcas' house. Dorcas' friends were weeping in her room. They showed Peter the clothes she had made for them.

Peter told them all to leave the room. He kneeled down and prayed, then turned to Dorcas and said, 'Get up.' She opened her eyes and when she saw Peter, she sat up. Peter took her hand and helped her out of bed. He called all her friends back.

'Here is Dorcas – well again.'

Many people believed in the Lord after they heard this amazing news.

THINK: We have heard so many amazing things about the Lord Jesus. We should believe in him too.

North of Joppa, in the town of Caesarea, lived a Roman soldier called Cornelius. He was a religious man who prayed regularly to God and who was kind to the poor. One afternoon he had a vision. He clearly saw an angel who said to him, 'Send to Joppa for Peter. He is staying with Simon, the tanner in his house by the sea.'

Cornelius sent two servants and a soldier to find Peter. When they arrived Peter was on the rooftop thinking about a vision he had received from the Lord, preparing him for this event. God the Holy Spirit instructed him to go with these men.

Peter went downstairs and said, 'I am the man you are looking for. Why have you come?'

'We have come from Cornelius, the centurion,' they replied. 'A holy angel told him to invite you to his house so that he could hear what you have to say.'

THINK: God arranged the meeting of Peter and Cornelius. He works in our lives too as we meet with people.

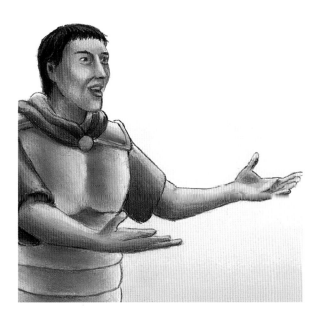

Peter invited Cornelius' servants into the house and they stayed there overnight. The next day Peter went from Joppa to Caesarea.

Cornelius was waiting for them. A large company of friends had gathered to hear God's message through Peter.

Peter preached, telling them that Jesus had followers from every nation. He told them about Jesus' miracles, his death and wonderful resurrection.

'Everyone who believes in him receives forgiveness of sin,' proclaimed Peter.

Cornelius and his friends believed the message and were filled with the Holy Spirit. They became followers of the Lord Jesus and were baptised.

THINK: It is our duty and privilege to believe God when we hear his message preached.

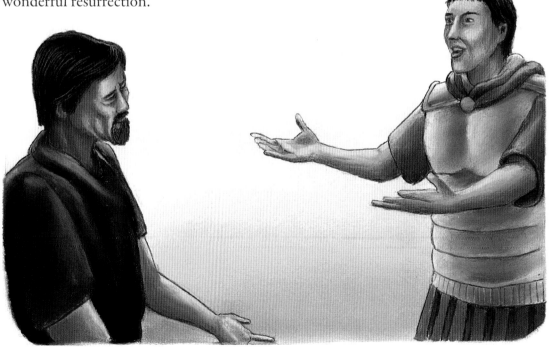

After Stephen's death many of the followers of Jesus were threatened with persecution too. They left Jerusalem and settled in different places like Cyprus and Antioch. Some preached the gospel not just to their fellow Jews but to Greeks also. The Lord blessed their work and many people believed the good news about Jesus and turned to the Lord.

When the church people in Jerusalem heard about this, they sent Barnabas to Antioch to find out what was happening. He saw for himself how God was working in Antioch. He encouraged the people to remain true to the Lord.

Barnabas went to Tarsus to ask Saul to come and help him. So for a whole year Barnabas and Saul worked with the church in Antioch, teaching and preaching.

The group of believers at Antioch were the first people to be called Christians.

PRAY: Thank the Lord for preachers and missionaries who teach God's Word to people all over the world.

King Herod hated the Christian church. He was very cruel – even putting some to death. He arrested Peter and had him thrown in prison – guarded by four groups of soldiers, four men in each group.

But Christian friends were praying earnestly for Peter. The night before he was due to go on trial, Peter was sleeping, chained between two soldiers. The prison was locked and guarded.

An angel of the Lord came to the prison and woke Peter up.

'Get up quickly,' he said. The chains fell from his hands. 'Get dressed and put on your sandals,' he added, 'and follow me.'

Peter did as he was told but he thought he was dreaming. Could this really be happening?

Past one guard they went, then another, right out into the street. Peter realised that God had delivered him from prison. He made his way to Mary's house.

THINK: Peter's situation seemed very difficult, but God was able to help him. He is able to help us too in all our problems.

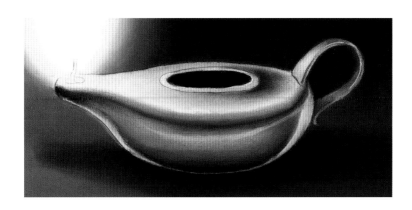

Many Christians had met in Mary's house to pray for Peter. A knock came to the outside door. A servant girl called Rhoda ran to answer it. She heard Peter's voice. She was so surprised that she did not open the door, but ran back inside to tell the others. 'Peter is at the door,' she exclaimed.

'Don't talk nonsense,' they said.

'It is Peter,' she insisted. 'I know his voice.'

Peter kept on knocking and eventually the door was opened. When they saw Peter, they were all amazed. He told them how the Lord had brought him out of prison. 'Go and tell my friends the good news.'

How pleased and thankful the people in Mary's house must have been that the Lord answered their prayer.

Peter then went away to a place where Herod would not find him.

PRAY: Be thankful to God for his answers to your prayers. He can answer prayers in simple ways and in amazing ways.

Saul's life was completely changed when he met the Lord Jesus on the road to Damascus. God used him to spread the gospel (the good news about Jesus' life, death and resurrection for his people) in many interesting places around the Mediterranean Sea. Even Saul's name changed. He was now known as Paul.

On the first trip Paul went with Barnabas, who had been his first friend in Jerusalem after his conversion, and a young helper, John Mark. They travelled through the island of Cyprus, preaching the gospel in the synagogue. They faced stiff opposition but God the Holy Spirit helped them to be strong. The governor of the island was so impressed by the teaching about the Lord that he believed in Jesus for himself.

From Cyprus they sailed across to the area we now call Turkey. John Mark left them at this point to go back home to Jerusalem.

THINK: Remember that God the Holy Spirit is always with the person who believes in Jesus Christ. He gives assurance and help and guidance.

Paul and Barnabas went from town to town preaching the good news about Jesus. Some listened eagerly but others chased them away.

At Lystra they met a crippled man who had never been able to walk. He listened intently as Paul spoke. When Paul looked at him, he knew that this man had faith to be healed so he called out, 'Stand up on your feet!'

Immediately the man jumped up and started to walk. The crowds watching were so impressed that they foolishly thought that Paul and Barnabas were gods. They wanted to worship them. This upset Paul and Barnabas very much.

'We are only men like you,' they protested. 'Do not worship us. Worship the living God who made the heavens and earth, and gives you everything you need.'

Even with these words they had difficulty in stopping the crowd from sacrificing to them.

THINK: God is the only one to be worshipped. It is right to say thank you to someone who has helped us, but never right to worship anyone apart from God the Father, the Son and the Holy Spirit.

Before long the mood of the crowd had completely changed, when some Jews started to speak against Paul and Barnabas. They won the crowd over to their point of view.

The crowd who had been worshipping Paul, now began to hurl stones at him.

He was dragged out of the city and left for dead.

Some believers came to his aid and Paul got up and went back into the city. The next day he and Barnabas left to preach in another city, Derbe.

On the return journey they stopped off at different towns, including Lystra. They encouraged the believers to remain true to the faith.

'We must go through many hardships to enter the kingdom of God,' Paul explained.

They appointed elders to look after the church, committing them to the Lord, before going on to the next place.

THINK: God is in control in every situation, even the most dangerous. Nothing could separate Paul from God's love.

Paul was joined by Silas for his next big trip. He returned to Lystra where he had been so badly treated, to encourage and strengthen the new believers who had come to know the Lord on Paul's first visit.

One of these Christians was a young man named Timothy. Timothy's mother, Eunice, and grandmother, Lois, had taught the Scriptures to him when he was a little boy. The elders of the church spoke well of Timothy, so Paul invited him to come and join them in their work.

The three men travelled together from town to town preaching and teaching. The churches were strengthened in their faith and grew in numbers every day.

PRAY: Thank God that faithful missionaries and preachers have taken his Word round the world and that God's message of salvation has reached you.

The Holy Spirit guided Paul and Barnabas and Timothy. He prevented them from going north into Bithynia and instead they went to the sea port of Troas.

During the night Paul had a vision. He saw a man from Macedonia standing and pleading with him, 'Come over to Macedonia, and help us.'

Immediately Paul and his companions got ready to sail over the sea to Macedonia in Europe. They believed God wanted them to preach the gospel there.

When they reached Philippi, the main city of the region, they stopped for several days.

PRAY: Be thankful to God for the people who teach you the Bible and tell you about the Saviour, the Lord Jesus Christ.

On the Sabbath day, they went out of the city to the riverside where they expected to find a quiet place to pray. Several women were meeting there and Paul preached the Word of God to the group.

Lydia was a business woman whose work was to sell beautiful purple cloth. She knew about God's Word, but on that day her heart was opened to respond quietly to Jesus Christ. She became a true believer.

She and her family were baptised. She persuaded Paul and his friends to come and stay at her house.

THINK: God worked gently in Lydia's life, making her respond to the love of Jesus Christ. God can change your heart too. Ask him to do this.

One day on the way to the prayer meeting, Paul met a slave girl who made lots of money for her owners by telling fortunes. An evil spirit made her do this. She kept following Paul and shouting out, 'These men are servants of God who are telling you the way to be saved.' At last Paul turned to her and commanded the evil spirit to come out of her.

At that moment the spirit left her. She could no longer tell fortunes. Her owners were very angry. They grabbed Paul and Silas and dragged them to the marketplace. They brought them before the judges and accused them of causing a disturbance in the town.

They were stripped and beaten and thrown into prison. The jailer was told to guard them carefully. They were put into the inner cell and their feet were fastened in the stocks. But even in prison Paul and Silas sang praise to God. Their trust was in the Lord God.

THINK: God can convert people who are in the grip of the devil. God is all-powerful. His love can reach the worst sinner.

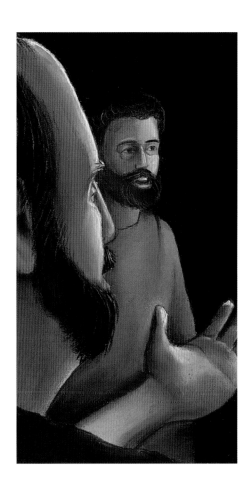

About midnight Paul and Silas were praying and singing praise to God from their prison cell. The other prisoners were listening to them.

Suddenly a violent earthquake shook the foundations of the prison, the doors flew open and all the chains came loose.

The jailer woke up and when he saw the doors open he was so afraid that his prisoners had escaped that he took out his sword and was about to kill himself. Just in time Paul shouted to him, 'Do not hurt yourself. We are all here.'

The jailer called for lights and hurried in to Paul and Silas. He brought them out of their cell and asked a very important question.

'Sirs, what must I do to be saved?'

'Believe in the Lord Jesus Christ and you will be saved,' was Paul's reply.

Paul and Silas explained to the jailer and his family the good news of the gospel of Jesus Christ. They all believed and were baptised.

THINK: Paul's message to the jailer is for us too. God's promise is true. Believe in the Lord Jesus Christ and you will be saved.

The jailer washed Paul and Silas's wounds and had a meal prepared for them.

The next day the judges sent officers to release Paul and Silas. 'You can go now,' they said.

'Not at all,' said Paul. 'We are Roman citizens and we have been beaten and thrown into jail without a trial. Let the judges come themselves and escort us out of prison.'

The judges were so embarrassed when they heard that Paul and Silas were Roman citizens. They rushed to take them from the jail and politely asked them to leave the city.

Before they left Philippi, Paul and Silas made a visit to Lydia's house where they met with the believers once again.

THINK: The new church at Philippi had three very different members – a slave girl, a wealthy business woman and the jailer from the prison. Jesus' love reaches out to all kinds of people and all are one in Christ Jesus.

Paul and his companions reached the city of Thessalonica. Paul preached in the synagogue explaining how Jesus Christ had suffered and died on the cross and had risen from the dead. Many people, both Jews and Greeks were convinced by Paul's teaching and believed in Jesus Christ. Some of the Jews were very jealous and rounded up some bad characters from the marketplace and started a riot in the city.

They rushed to Jason's house where they thought they might find Paul and Silas, but when they did not find them there they dragged Jason out and got him into trouble with the city officials. Under darkness of night Paul and Silas left Thessalonica.

THINK: It is not easy to follow Jesus. Just as people hated Jesus they will hate his followers also. But the Lord has promised to be with his people always.

Paul and Silas went straight to the Jewish synagogue when they arrived in Berea. The people there were keen to hear Paul's message and they checked up in the Scriptures every day to make sure that what Paul was saying was true. Many became believers in Jesus Christ.

The same Jews that had caused trouble in Thessalonica came to Berea to stir up opposition to Paul and his preaching. Paul was advised to leave immediately and some friends escorted him to Athens on the coast.

Silas and Timothy stayed in Berea, but Paul sent back word to them to join him in Athens as soon as possible.

PRAY: Thank God for giving you his Word. Ask him to help you to read it with eagerness every day.

In Athens Paul was upset to see so many people worshipping idols. Every day he would debate with the religious people in the synagogue and in the marketplace with anyone who happened to be there.

The educated men of Athens loved to discuss new ideas and they were interested to hear what Paul had to say. Paul stood up in their meeting place and told them about the great God who had made the heavens and the earth and yet has a care for every person. He warned them that God commands everyone to repent of their sins and that God will judge the world justly.

When Paul told them that Jesus Christ had risen from the dead, some of the listeners sneered but others wanted to hear more about it. A few people did truly believe the message of the gospel that Paul preached.

THINK: Jesus' resurrection is an important part of the gospel message. By this, God declared Jesus to be his Son and confirmed that he accepted Christ's sacrifice for sin on the cross.

335. Paul at Corinth - Acts 18

When Paul left Athens he headed to Corinth. He stayed in the home of Priscilla and Aquila who were tent makers like Paul. He worked with them for a while. He was joined by Silas and Timothy. Paul devoted himself then to preaching to the Jews about Jesus Christ. Some of them started to insult Paul. 'From now on, I will just preach to the Gentiles,' said Paul.

So Paul no longer went to the synagogue but instead preached in the house next door. Some whole families heard the Word there and believed and were baptised. One night God spoke to Paul in a dream telling him not to be afraid. 'Keep on speaking my message,' God said. 'I am with you. No one will harm you. I have many people in this city.'

So Paul stayed for a year-and-a-half teaching the Word of God.

THINK: God has many people all over the world. He is building his church every day – adding to the number of those who trust in him.

Aquila and Priscilla went with Paul on the next stage of his journey to Ephesus, where Paul left them as he carried on to Caesarea.

Aquila and Priscilla served the Lord in Ephesus. They heard a man called Apollos fervently preaching in the synagogue. He had a great knowledge of God's Word, but some of his views, especially about baptism, were not right.

Priscilla and Aquila asked Apollos to come to their house. They spent some time with him explaining the Word of God more fully. As a result, Apollos became a much more useful preacher of God's Word. He was able to successfully debate with the Jews, proving from the Scriptures that Jesus was the Christ, the promised one from God.

PRAY: Say thank you to God for giving you his Word, the Bible, which tells us about his Son who came to our world and was called Jesus, the Saviour.

351

Paul returned to Ephesus and worked there for over two years. His preaching had a great effect on many people, but some objected strongly so Paul moved to another hall. They had discussions there every day. Many heard the Word of God and followed Jesus.

God did many miracles through Paul. Some people were healed of illness and evil spirits were cast out.

Some who had formerly practiced evil sorcery gathered together all their evil scrolls and publicly burned them, even although they were valuable.

This showed how God's Word grew in power and spread in the town.

PRAY: Pray that God's Word would be preached where you live and that many would trust in Jesus.

A silversmith called Demetrius stirred up trouble. He was annoyed that Paul's preaching had turned people away from worshipping idols. They no longer bought the silver shrines that he made.

So with other silversmiths he caused a riot. They shouted abuse about Paul and his friends and would not listen to anyone.

Eventually the city clerk made them see sense. 'They have done nothing to harm you. If you have any grievance, take it to the law courts in a civil manner. Don't start a riot.'

The crowd dispersed. When it was all over, Paul preached a farewell message and left the town.

He set off to Greece and Macedonia preaching and encouraging the believers along the way.

THINK: We should not be surprised that there is opposition to the truth today. Ask God to keep you strong by trusting in Jesus.

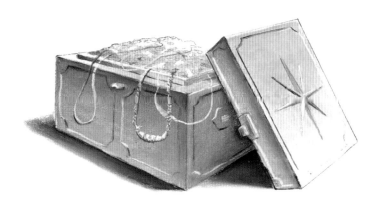

Paul and his companions stayed at Troas for a week. The Lord's Day evening before they were due to leave, Paul preached in an upstairs room. A boy called Eutychus sat on a window ledge listening.

Paul had so much to say to the people before he would leave them that he talked until midnight. Eutychus was so tired, he drifted off into a deep sleep and fell right down to the ground from the upstairs window.

He was picked up dead, but Paul came down and threw himself on the young man, putting his arms around him. 'Don't be alarmed,' he said. 'He's all right.' And so he was. Eutychus was brought back to life by the power of God.

Everyone went back upstairs again, shared bread together and carried on speaking till dawn.

Paul then had to leave them and Eutychus went home safe and well.

THINK: It is good for us to gather together with God's people on his special day to worship him and to hear the gospel preached.

Paul wanted to get back to Jerusalem in time to celebrate the Feast of Pentecost. He stopped off at various places on the route to meet with the believers. The Christians at Tyre advised Paul not to go to Jerusalem, but at the end of the week he carried on.

At Caesarea he visited Philip's home for several days. A prophet named Agabus arrived from Judea. He took Paul's belt and tied up his own feet and hands with it. 'This is God the Holy Spirit's message for you,' he told Paul. 'If you go to Jerusalem this is what will happen to you. You will be captured by the Jews and handed over to the Romans.'

Paul's friends begged him not to go to Jerusalem. 'Why are you crying?' he asked. 'I am ready not only to be put in prison in Jerusalem but to die for the sake of the Lord Jesus.'

Paul was determined to go to Jerusalem.

PRAY: Pray for the people who are facing danger and even death today because they love and follow Jesus. Ask that they would keep faithful to the Lord.

Soon after Paul arrived in Jerusalem he met the leaders of the church and reported in detail what God had done through his ministry. The elders praised God for this.

At the suggestion of the elders, Paul agreed to go to the temple to show he respected the Jewish customs.

The Jewish Christians in Jerusalem were careful to follow the laws of Moses. He did not want to offend them.

Paul went next day to the temple for a ceremony to indicate he would offer a sacrifice seven days later. Before the seven days had passed, some of his enemies recognised him and roused a mob. 'This is the man who tells everybody to disobey our laws,' they shouted. The whole city was in uproar.

Paul was dragged out of the temple and beaten.

THINK: God is always with his people even when life is difficult. Nothing can separate them from the love of God.

The commander of the Roman army heard that the whole city was in uproar because of Paul. He immediately gathered some soldiers and ran to see what was happening. When the rioters saw the soldiers, they immediately stopped beating Paul.

The commander arrested Paul and ordered him to be bound by two chains. (Agabus' prophecy had come true). He questioned the onlookers but could make no sense of their answers. One shouted one thing and one shouted another. He ordered that Paul should be taken to the barracks, rescuing him from the angry mob. He had to be carried by the soldiers for his own safety.

THINK: Jesus Christ is king and is in control of all his people and all that happens to them. What a comfort for Paul and for us.

Paul asked, 'May I speak?' With the commander's permission, he spoke to the crowd telling them his life story and how he was converted. The crowd listened quietly until he said, 'The Lord told me to go far away to reach the Gentiles.'

This angered them and they shouted insults again.

'Take him away,' ordered the commander, 'and flog him.'

As they were about to beat Paul, he asked a soldier, 'Is it legal for you to flog a Roman citizen who has not been found guilty?'

The soldier reported this to the commander, who came to investigate.

'Are you a Roman citizen?' he asked Paul. 'I had to pay a large sum of money for my citizenship.'

'But I was born a citizen,' Paul replied.

The commander was alarmed when he realised how badly he had treated Paul, a Roman citizen.

THINK: The Lord Jesus suffered more than any other man. He was forsaken by God the Father as he took the punishment for the sin of his people.

The next day the commander brought Paul before the Jewish council to find out what was causing the problem.

Paul had a good idea. Knowing that the council members were not all of the same mind on the matter, Paul announced loudly, 'I am being tried here today because I believe in the resurrection (or rising again) of the dead.' This remark divided the council so they began to argue among themselves. The dispute became so violent that the commander was afraid Paul would be pulled to pieces by them. He ordered the soldiers to take him back to the barracks.

The Lord spoke to Paul that night. 'Take courage. Just as you have spoken for me here in Jerusalem, so you must also speak in Rome.'

THINK: Jesus is with us too and tells us to be courageous and remember that our future is in his hands. Jesus rose from the dead and so those who believe in him will rise to eternal life.

345. A Conspiracy to Kill Paul - Acts 23

The next morning over forty men vowed together not to eat or drink anything until they had killed Paul. The plan was to get Paul back to the council for more questioning and kill him on the way.

Paul's nephew heard about this plot and bravely came to the barracks to warn Paul. Paul asked a soldier to take the boy to the commander.

'This boy has something important to tell you,' the soldier said. The commander took the boy by the hand and asked, 'What do you want to tell me?'

'The Jews are going to ask you to take Paul back to the council tomorrow. Don't do it. There will be an ambush of over forty men waiting to kill him.'

'Don't tell anyone that you have reported this to me,' said the commander as the boy left.

The commander immediately acted on this information.

THINK: Ask Jesus to make you brave enough to do the right thing in the playground or school or at home.

The commander gave the order. 'Get ready 200 soldiers, 70 horsemen and 200 spearsmen for ten o'clock tonight. Get a horse for Paul to ride and transfer him safely to Governor Felix in Caesarea.'

The commander wrote a letter to Felix explaining what had happened, and that he was passing the case on to him.

Under cover of darkness the armed guard took Paul as far as Antipatras. They returned to barracks next morning, leaving the horsemen to take Paul on to Caesarea.

There Paul and the letter were presented to the governor. After he read the letter, Felix just said, 'I will deal with your case later, when your accusers come.'

So Paul was kept as a prisoner in the palace.

THINK: Paul had to be patient as he waited for his case to be dealt with. Pray that God would give you patience to wait for his perfect timing in the events of your life.

When Ananias, the high priest, arrived with other leaders, Paul was brought out to stand trial before Felix. The lawyer, Tertullus, put the case against Paul, accusing him of being a troublemaker all over the world.

Paul was given the right to reply, assuring Felix that he was not guilty of any of their accusations.

'What I will admit,' he said, 'is that I worship the God of our fathers and believe in the way of salvation.'

Felix did not know what to do. He ordered Paul back to prison but told the guards to be gentle with him and to allow him visitors.

He invited Paul to preach to himself and his wife, Drusilla, about faith in Jesus Christ. Felix was terrified when Paul spoke about righteousness and judgement to come. 'Go away now and when it is more convenient I will call for you.'

But he never did.

THINK: God warns us not to put off thinking about him. 'Now is the day of salvation,' he says.

Two years later a new governor took over from Felix. He was called Festus.

On a visit to Jerusalem, Festus was approached by the Jewish leaders who begged him to bring Paul for trial there. But Festus refused.

Back at Caesarea the court was set up again. The Jews from Jerusalem hurled their usual accusations which Paul firmly denied.

To please the Jews, Festus asked Paul, 'Are you willing to go to Jerusalem to stand trial?'

'No,' said Paul. 'I demand my right of appearing before the Emperor himself. I appeal to Caesar.'

Festus conferred with his advisors and then announced, 'Very well. You have appealed to Caesar. You shall go to Caesar.'

THINK: Paul knew it was more important to live to please God rather than other people. Ask God to help you to obey him and his Word. This is pleasing to him.

A few days later King Agrippa arrived with Bernice to visit Festus. They discussed Paul's case. 'I would like to hear him for myself,' said King Agrippa.

The next day Paul was brought before King Agrippa. 'I don't think he has done anything worthy of death,' said Festus, 'but he has appealed to Caesar.'

'Tell us your story,' said Agrippa to Paul.

Paul told him about his life and how he had become a Christian and spent his time preaching the gospel in many places.

Agrippa interrupted Paul. 'Do you think you can persuade me to become a Christian?'

'I would wish that you and everyone in this room would be like me,' replied Paul.

Afterwards Agrippa and Festus agreed that Paul had done nothing worthy of death or imprisonment.

'He could have been set free, if he had not appealed to Caesar,' said Agrippa.

THINK: Paul preached faithfully to Agrippa, but only God the Holy Spirit can change the heart. Remember the story Jesus told about the sower – not every seed planted was fruitful.

So Paul set sail for Rome under the charge of a Roman centurion called Julius. The ship put into shore at Sidon and Paul was allowed to go and visit his friends. The route took them north of Cyprus and at Myra in Asia they changed ships.

Progress was slow and difficult as the wind kept blowing them off course. The journey was becoming more and more dangerous.

At the harbour of Fair Havens on the island of Crete, Paul warned Julius. 'I can see this voyage ending in disaster. We should stay here.'

But Julius did not want to stay all winter there. He did not listen to Paul's advice. The decision was taken to sail on.

In the middle of the Adriatic Sea they hit a big storm. The ship could make no headway and was tossed about with hurricane force winds. The ship's lifeboat had to be hoisted from the water to stop it being shattered. The sailors started to throw some cargo overboard to lighten the load.

THINK: God is with his people in the storm and in the calm. He has promised never to leave us or forsake us.

Everyone on board was sure they would perish – except Paul. 'Don't despair,' he urged. 'None of us will be lost. Only the ship will be destroyed. An angel of the Lord spoke to me last night and told me that the lives on the ship will be spared. I have faith in God that it will happen as he told me.'

After fourteen nights out in the open sea the sailors sensed they were nearing land. They took soundings and sure enough the sea was becoming shallower. Now the danger of being wrecked on the rocks was looming closer.

The sailors dropped four anchors from the stern of the boat and prayed for daylight. They thought they would make a break for it and tried to put the lifeboat into the sea while pretending to work at the anchors.

Paul boldly confronted the centurion. 'Unless these men stay with the ship, we will not be saved.'

So the soldiers cut the ropes of the lifeboat and tossed it into the sea.

THINK: Paul was confident in God, no matter what happened. He had faith to believe God's promise. Pray that God would give you faith in Christ alone.

Before dawn Paul urged everyone to have something to eat. 'You have been under such stress for fourteen days that you have not eaten anything. You need food to survive.'

He took some bread, gave thanks to God for it and the others took courage from him and did the same. When daylight came they could see a bay with a sandy beach. Before the ship could reach the shore it became stuck in a sandbar. The ship was broken in pieces by the pounding waves.

The soldiers planned to kill the prisoners to prevent them from escaping. The centurion wanted to keep Paul alive, so he forbade them.

Those who could swim jumped overboard and made for land. The others kept afloat on planks and broken pieces of the ship.

All reached land safely, just as God had told Paul.

PRAY: Be thankful that our gracious, all-powerful God always keeps his promises.

When they reached land they discovered that the island was Malta. The islanders treated them so kindly. They built a big fire on the shore to warm themselves because of the cold and rain.

Paul gathered a pile of brushwood and as he put it on the fire, a snake appeared and attached itself to his hand. The islanders thought this was a sign that Paul must be a murderer.

When Paul shook the snake off into the fire and was none the worse, they changed their minds and thought he was a god.

The chief official of Malta entertained them in his own home. His father was sick in bed. Paul prayed for him and placed his hands on him and he was healed.

Many others then came to Paul and were also cured of their illnesses.

When they were at last ready to leave for Rome, the people of Malta showed more kindness by giving them supplies for the journey.

THINK: God had power to protect Paul from the snake and to heal the sick people. He is the same powerful God today. Trust him for everything.

After three months in Malta another ship was ready to take Paul and the others to Rome. The sea voyage ended in Puteoli over 100 miles south of Rome. They stayed there for a week with some friends before travelling on by road to Rome.

The Christians in Rome got word that Paul was coming so they travelled out of town to meet him. Paul was greatly encouraged and thanked God for their love and support.

In Rome, Paul was allowed to live by himself in a house with a soldier to guard him.

He was able to have visitors and for two years could carry on preaching the gospel to all who came to see him. Some who heard the gospel believed on the Lord Jesus Christ.

Paul also wrote many letters to the new churches that he set up.

THINK: Many hard experiences brought Paul to Rome. Remember that all things work together for good to those who love God.

6. Epistles, Revelation and God's Word

Books of the Bible:

1st and 2nd Corinthians, Ephesians,
Philippians, 1st and 2nd Thessalonians,
1st and 2nd Timothy, Philemon,
Hebrews, James, Revelation.

What you will read about:

Paul's Letters to the Churches,
John's Vision, The Trinity,
Jesus the Sin Bearer,
The Bible - The Best Book of All.

Paul wrote two letters to the church in Corinth to encourage them in their Christian life and to correct them for some wrong ideas they had.

Paul explains how important love is. Even if someone could speak in any language, or knew everything there was to know or had amazing faith, if he did not show love, it would be worth nothing. Even if a man gives all his money to the poor, without love it is of no value.

Paul gives a beautiful description of love. There is also a description of the person who shows love. Does it describe you? Can you put your name in the place of 'love'?

Love is very patient and kind, never envious, never boastful or proud. Love is not rude, does not get angry easily. Love does not hold grudges. Love is never glad about evil but is happy when truth wins its way. Faith, hope and love are all wonderful things but the greatest one is love.

THINK: Remember that if we love God, it is because he has first loved us.

In the letter to the church at Ephesus, Paul gives lots of good advice and teaching about Jesus Christ. The children, who were part of the church in Ephesus, were reminded to obey their parents as the commandments say.

Paul warned the Christians about the wicked schemes of the devil and told them how to stand up against him. Paul told them to be strong in the Lord and his power. Just as a soldier has armour to protect him so a Christian has God's armour. Put on the belt of truth around your waist, and the breastplate of righteousness. Wear shoes that will fit you with readiness to preach the gospel of peace. Use the shield of faith to stop the fiery darts of Satan. Put on the helmet of salvation to protect you. Use the sword of the Spirit to attack the devil. The sword is the Bible, the Word of God.

THINK: Keep praying all the time, asking God for all you need. Use the Word of God to help you to resist the devil and he will flee from you.

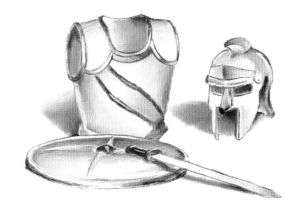

After Paul left Thessalonica he did not forget the believers who belonged to the church there. He kept in touch by writing letters.

Paul assured them that he always prayed for them. He told them he thanked God for their work and faithfulness.

He longed to see them again but was glad that Timothy had brought him good news of his visit. Paul urged them to live holy lives and to be ready for the time when Jesus would return to earth. Paul knew that his work needed God's help. He asked the Thessalonian Christians to pray for him – that the message he preached in other places would prosper just as it did with them.

THINK: We can take every problem and worry to the Lord in prayer. Nothing is too big for him. Nothing is too little to take to him.

The church at Philippi received a lovely letter from Paul and his helper, Timothy. The church in Philippi was the first one in Europe.

Paul tells them how thankful he is to God for them. It gave him great joy to pray for the Philippian church. He felt they were partners with him in the gospel work. They provided for him in practical ways when he was in need.

'Don't be anxious about anything,' Paul urged them. 'Pray to God about everything and rejoice and be thankful whatever your circumstances. Then the peace of God will keep your minds.'

Paul encouraged them to be like Christ who was so humble that he even went to the cross to die for his people. But God has exalted him. At his name, Jesus, every knee will bow one day and every tongue confess that Jesus Christ is Lord.

THINK: Remember to pray for the preacher in your church. Ask God to bless the gospel of Jesus preached to you and others.

Paul wrote two letters to a young pastor, Timothy, who had travelled with him and helped to spread the gospel.

Paul encouraged Timothy to preach the Word of God at all times, rebuking sin and encouraging the study of the truth.

Paul emphasised the importance of the Scriptures, God's Word, which Timothy had been taught as a little boy by his mother, Eunice, and grandmother, Lois. All Scripture is given to us by the inspiration of God and is so valuable to tell us what is true, to correct us when we go wrong, and to teach us how to live.

Timothy was not a very strong person, but Paul urged him to be strong with the strength that Jesus Christ gives. He told him that training to be godly was far more important than physical training. Even though he was young, Timothy set a good example for the church.

THINK: The Bible teaches us how to live. If we delight in God's law we will be like a tree by a river – fruitful and healthy.

360. The Runaway Slave and His Master - Philemon

Philemon was a wealthy Christian in Colosse. He had a large house with slaves. One slave, Onesimus, ran away after stealing from Philemon. This was a serious offence worthy of severe punishment.

Onesimus fled to Rome where he met Paul and heard God's way of salvation from him. He came to trust in the Lord Jesus too.

Paul wrote a letter to Philemon asking him to forgive Onesimus, and accept him back as a Christian brother. Paul offered to pay anything that Onesimus owed.

Onesimus had run away to escape justice, but the grace of God changed his life and he returned to Philemon as his brother in the Lord.

THINK: Grace is the undeserved love of God to sinners, because of what Jesus Christ has done. God's grace saved Onesimus from slavery to sin and can save you too.

James, a half-brother of Jesus, wrote to God's people all over the world with good advice about how a Christian should live.

James advised us to be careful about our speech. 'Be quick to listen, slow to speak and slow to become angry.'

The tongue is a very small part of our body yet it can cause great damage or be a great influence for good. It is like the bit in a horse's mouth which can cause a huge horse to turn one way or another. A big ship can be steered by a very small rudder.

It only takes one small spark to set on fire a huge forest. One false or unwise remark can cause untold damage.

It is more difficult to control our tongue than to control a wild animal.

PRAY: Ask the Lord to help you to control your tongue and to forgive you when you say something sinful.

The apostle John wrote the book of Revelation while he was a prisoner for his faith on the island of Patmos. He was an old man by this time. Many Christians were treated cruelly or even killed by the cruel Roman emperor.

One Lord's Day (Sunday) the Lord Jesus himself appeared to John. John was amazed at his dazzling glory. The Lord spoke to him and told him to write it all down. God had special messages for each of the seven churches of Asia – Ephesus, Smyrna, Pergamum, Thyatira, Sardis, Philadelphia and Laodicea. He encouraged the churches but also corrected them lovingly.

THINK: John's book of Revelation is full of word pictures. One is of a Lamb who was killed, and received power and glory from God. The Lamb is a symbol for the Lord Jesus Christ, which reminds us of John the Baptist pointing to Jesus, the Lamb of God, who takes away the sin of the world.

John saw a vision of heaven and he described what he saw. In heaven there will be no tears, no death, no sorrow, no crying, no pain. The city wall is of jasper, a precious stone. The city is made of pure gold. The foundations of the city are adorned with precious jewels. The twelve gates are made of pearls. The street is pure gold. John did not see a temple in his vision of the city because the Lord Almighty and the Lamb (Jesus Christ) are the temple.

There was no need for sun or moon because the glory of God illuminated it.

Nothing wicked will enter heaven – only those whose names are written in the Lamb's book of life – those who are trusting in Christ alone for salvation.

Jesus will return one day. He will judge the world and take his people to be with himself in heaven.

THINK: If you are trusting in Jesus, God has promised that you will be in heaven with him.

The Bible tells us that there is only one God. There are three different persons in this one God, God the Father, God the Son and God the Holy Spirit. They exist together but we must worship them as one God.

Our world was created by God. The first words of the Bible are 'In the beginning God ...' He has existed from all eternity. John speaks of the Son of God as the Word who was God and with God the Father in the beginning. The world was created by the Word that God spoke. When the world was empty and formless, God the Spirit was hovering over the waters.

So the three persons who are the one God were involved in the creation of the world and of people. 'Let us make man in our image, like ourselves,' said God, as he made the first man Adam.

This is a great mystery which should make us worship God.

THINK: There is only one true and living God. However there are three persons in this one God. They are one God, the same in substance and equal in power and glory.

Sin spoiled God's perfect world. Everyone is a sinner.

God had a wonderful plan to save his people from sin. All through their history, God taught the people of Israel about his plan. He instructed them to make sacrifices of unblemished animals because they were sinners. The blood of these animals could not take away sin. But it was a picture of what would happen in the future when God's Son would die for sinners. His sacrifice would be the perfect sacrifice.

The Lord Jesus Christ came into the world to be the real and only worthwhile sacrifice for sin. His sacrifice did not need to be repeated again and again. He died once and for all, on the cross at Calvary.

God looks on Jesus' perfect sacrifice for those who trust him, and forgives their sins. 'I will remember them no more,' he says.

THINK: Thank God for Jesus, the most wonderful gift of all.

The Bible is a very special book, written by many different men, all inspired by God. God is the author, and he makes no mistakes. His Word is powerful. How thankful we should be that God has preserved his Word down through the ages and that we can read it today. Jesus told us that God's Word would remain for ever.

The Bible is like a lamp giving light and guidance on our journey through life. The Bible is like a sword, a mighty weapon to help us fight against our enemy, the devil. The Bible is like food – milk for a little baby or meat for a big man – the nourishment needed for our souls no matter how young or old we are.

The Bible teaches the truth, shows us what is wrong in our lives, corrects us and helps us to do what is right.

THINK: The Bible is the power of God for salvation for all who trust in the Lord Jesus Christ.

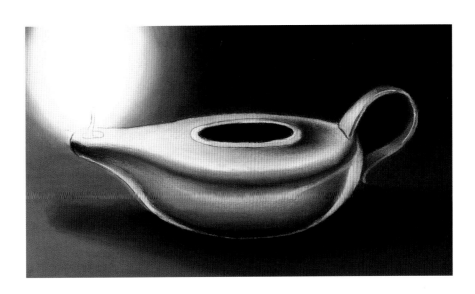

CHRISTIAN FOCUS PUBLICATIONS

Christian Focus | Christian Heritage | CF4K | Mentor

Christian Focus Publications publishes books for adults and children under its four main imprints: Christian Focus, Christian Heritage, CF4K and Mentor. Our books reflect that God's Word is reliable and Jesus is the way to know him, and live for ever with him.

Our children's publication list includes a Sunday school curriculum that covers pre-school to early teens; puzzle and activity books. We also publish personal and family devotional titles, biographies and inspirational stories that children will love.

If you are looking for quality Bible teaching for children then we have an excellent range of Bible story and age specific theological books. From pre-school to teenage fiction, we have it covered!

C F 4 • K
Because you're never too young to know Jesus

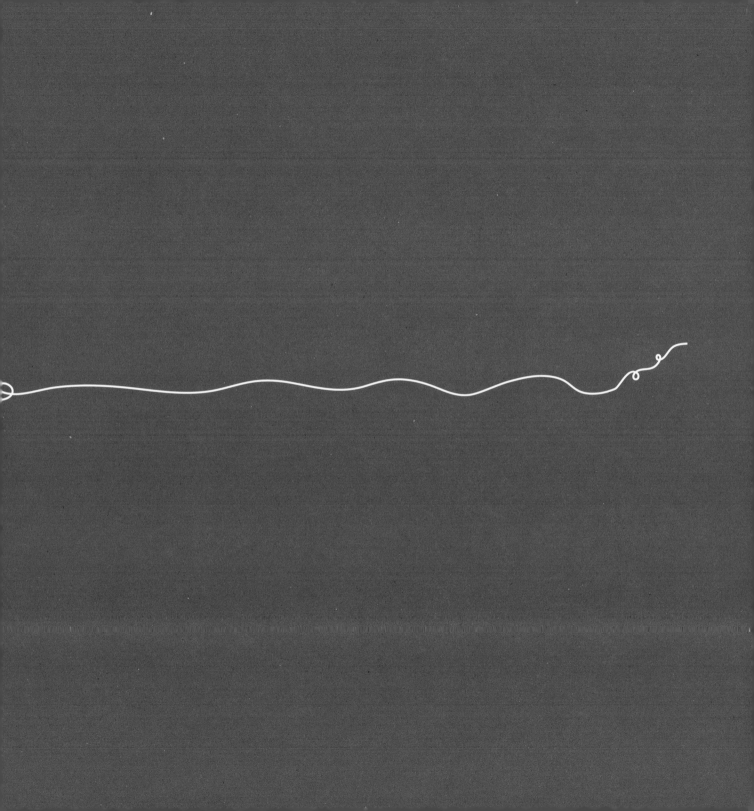

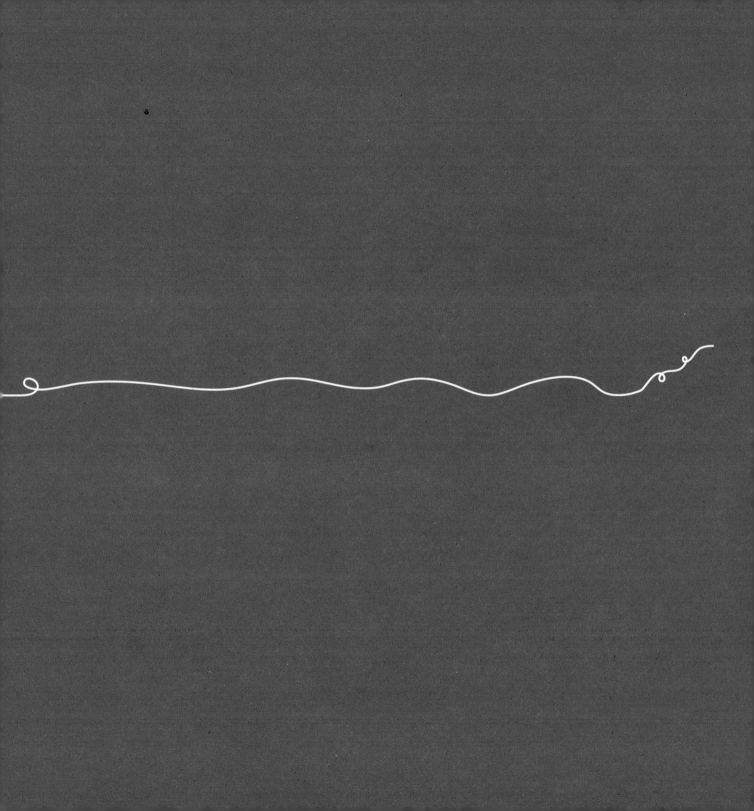